LIFE IN THE OVERLAP

JEAN DARNALL

Life In The Overlap

LAKELAND
Marshall Pickering
3 Beggarwood Lane,
Baskingstoke, Hants RG23 7LP

Copyright © Christian Life College 1977
First Published 1977
Reprinted 1979
This edition printed 1985

ISBN 0 551 00786 9

Printed in Great Britain by
Hunt Barnard Printing Ltd.,
Aylesbury, Bucks.
9760M50

Thanks to Elmer. He suggested the format of this book — a true life story followed by biblical truth. Living with him in the Overlap is an exciting experience in marriage.

Thanks to our son John. His drawings are windows in the structure so you can see through what I have written.

Thanks to La Donna whose ministry in England contributed one of the most stirring stories in this book.

Thanks to God for his Word. The Guide to Life in the Overlap at the back of this book will live long after I have moved out of the Overlap. I hope every reader will discover the treasure there.

Contents

1
Life in the Overlap

The long dreary Oval Station platform was empty. At either end of the cave-like hole the underground train tracks stretched into the black tunnel. I waited in the gloomy silence for my train. Suddenly the sharp clicking sound of a girl hurrying down the steps from the street above vibrated down the empty platform.

'Oh, I'm glad you're still here.' She was out of breath. 'I hoped I'd find you.'

She was one of the first year students in my evening class at Christian Life College, across the street at St Mark's Church.

'Hello, Jill.' She looked upset. Her dark eyes pleaded for my attention.

'Jean, I need to talk to you. I have had such a lot of problems since I started college.'

'Better hurry . . .' I felt the cool air blowing in my face, forced through the tube like a vanguard ahead of the coming train.

'What's your station?' Jill asked.

'Regent's Park is closest home.'

'Oh, I'm going the other way . . . Well, I don't know . . .' Jill was confused by the approaching train.

'I'll talk to you more at college,' I quickly assured her. 'Tomorrow night, definitely.'

'O.K., but you know what?' Her voice rose above

the noise of the train. 'I thought that when I became a Christian all my problems would be solved.'

The train was slowing down. I moved towards the doors. Jill rushed on, walking beside me. 'You know what's happened? I've exchanged one set of problems for another.'

The train screeched to a stop. The glass doors slid open with a bang. A few passengers automatically looked up. I stepped aboard and turned, calling out to Jill, 'You're right, you know. Exactly right. You just gave a concise definition of the Christian life ... another set of problems.'

The doors slammed shut. Jill stepped back, looking puzzled. She slowly waved as the train pulled me into the tunnel. I sank down into the nearest seat, relieved.

I knew Jill would catch me up. When I passed her in the hall at the college I knew she had a problem. Even before that, I knew. In class she had not listened while I was teaching. She was nervous, under strain. I noticed how she kept chewing her lower lip, looking down, avoiding the questions, never looking me in the eyes. It annoyed me. Later, when I passed her in the hall I said hello, but I knew I hadn't given her a chance to get past the greeting. She wanted to say more, but I had hurried on murmuring something about my train. I left her standing there, but as I hurried across the street to the Oval Underground Station I was sure that she would catch up with me. I could just see her. She'd stand there a moment, undecided. Then, she'd suddenly start running after me. I had felt her coming.

Why had I hurried on and left her at Christian Life College? I knew she wanted to talk. I was tired for one thing, not just physically tired, but tired of seeing defeated Christians with all their weak spots showing. Tired of Christians who kept coming back for more prayer; who never seemed to get over the top and win, but were trapped in a trench of unending war. They not only had problems, but their problems had them by the throat.

While I rode home on the tube I remembered how a counsellor at a youth camp last summer had complained: 'I wish there was something we could do about defeated Christians; you know, those problem people. They mess up the scene you preachers set up on victorious Christian living (a subject we had been teaching all through the camp). Wish we could put them backstage, out of sight.'

'Well, if we did that the cast would be considerably reduced,' I thought. 'They don't keep out of sight, they keep coming ...'

When we met the next evening, Jill was apologetic.

'I guess you must think I'm bad news, coming to you with my problems. I hate to bother a busy person like you.' She needed reassurance.

'Jill, I'm glad you came.' Inwardly I felt a twinge of guilt, recalling how I had dodged her the night before. But now I was ready to help her.

'I just had to talk to you,' she continued. 'I feel such a hypocrite, pretending I have no problems, when I do.'

'Jill, when we admit we have problems, we take our first step towards inner peace. Confession is the best way to change our conflicts into conquests. That's how we solve our problems. The day I started coming out with the truth about my inner conflicts, was the day I began to understand myself and others a lot better. I'm still learning how to handle inner conflict and I suppose I'll go on for the rest of my life.'

Jill's face brightened. 'I'm encouraged, but I'm surprised to hear you say you have problems. Your life seems like one miracle after another. I wish I had victory. I'm defeated. Why is it so hard for me to live the Christian life?'

'I think it is partly due to what you know and partly due to what you don't know.'

She looked a little puzzled, but leaned back to listen.

'I think that Christians are disillusioned rather than defeated. For instance, you've come to Christian Life College with high expectations. Perhaps you thought that once you started here you wouldn't have so many problems. But being a Christian does not insulate us from difficulties. Anyone who thinks so will be shattered when they find they have some of the same problems they had before they were Christians.'

'And some new ones, too,' Jill added.

I remembered how she had said the night before, 'I've changed one set of problems for another.'

'One of the reasons for this disillusionment is that a lot of strong, positive teaching and testimony produce an incomplete picture of the Christian life. It's all promises of blessings, and no warnings of the battles. When the problems come, the believer compares ideal biblical revelation with his own human experiences and can't bring the two together. So what he knows defeats him, because of what he doesn't know.'

We both laughed at my double Dutch.

'Jill, you are right when you say that you've exchanged one set of problems for another, but don't forget that there is a great difference in the outcome of those problems. The problems of life are dead-end streets ending in defeat. The problems of the new life are avenues that lead us from victory to victory into the purposes of God. Those purposes are eternal.'

She looked troubled, remembering what she had

12

come to tell me. 'I find it very hard to see any good purpose in the problems I've got.'

As we talked I discovered Jill was nearly demolished by conflicts that centred around her home, her job and our college. She taught at a London school on the south side of the Thames. She was at the point of giving up her job and she wanted to leave Christian Life College. She felt zero, a non-success, in everything. She was close to complete defeat.

'I feel there's no use. I can't see anything to do but get out and go away from it all.'

Looking at Jill, so small and miserable, I wondered where she would go. I'd seen the sad evidence of those who had gone backwards. I recalled the former alcoholic who began to drink again. There was the middle-aged woman salvaged from a ship-wrecked life of broken morals, who allowed herself to drift dangerously close to the currents of uncontrolled passion. I remembered the former incurable who gratefully received a miracle in answer to prayer, yet later doubted it, even denied it. Where did they go?

The apostle Peter felt so deeply about the return of a man to his former sinful life that he compared the act to that of a dog returning to its vomit. Sickening. The allegory was purposely ridiculous. Peter, when asked by Jesus if he would go back, replied, 'Go back? To what? Where do we go?'

Some of Jill's problems were legacies of the past and some had developed since she had committed her life to Christ, five years before.

Her home was an area of conflict; mother and father quarrelling almost constantly. Her mother resented it when Jill's alcoholic father showed her any love at all. When he drank he treated Jill to all kinds of gifts and showed his affection. Her mother would object and the fight would start, lasting long after he'd sobered up. Jill rarely spoke up, but kept out of the way. She stayed late at school, visited friends and finally got a job that kept her away as much as possible.

Then a friend at work led Jill to Christ.

'Jill, why did you decide to become a Christian?' I asked.

She hesitated, thinking over my question. 'I came to Jesus hoping to get away from my problems, I suppose. I yearned to have a different life, to be happy. I guess I expected I wouldn't have the old troubles. I felt guilty, too, about a lot of things. Were those the wrong motives for becoming a Christian, Jean?'

'We all usually start out with some motives just about like yours, but then, as we go on with the Lord, our motives should change. We mature.'

Jill went on with her story.

'My mother was furious when I told her that I'd committed my life to the Lord. She mocked me and predicted that I would fail. She shouted at me, "You'll never be a good Christian. You're a liar. Nobody will believe a liar like you." '

Jill didn't know why her mother called her a liar. She was always saying it. A year after her conversion Jill decided the Lord wanted her to be a school teacher. She worked hard, finally finishing her training in spite of her mother's objections. Her dad died while she was at teacher training college.

She decided to come to London and was given a position at a south-side school. Travelling down from the north country she settled into lodgings near Kennington. One of our students lived near and told her about the evening classes at Christian Life College. After prayer she came to an interview and was accepted.

I failed to see why she should be so troubled.

'For one thing, it seems like you've been led of the Lord, Jill. What's the problem?'

'There are some things I can't forget,' she said. When I left to go to teacher training college, my mother started her usual unjust accusations. She went into a rage. My dad was awfully sick then. His lungs were bad. I could see our quarrel was upsetting him. He began to cough, and had a terrible spasm. I got angry and all the hate I had in me erupted, just like a volcano. I exploded. I didn't know I had such terrible feelings and words in me. They boiled over. My mother didn't stop. She screamed louder than ever, but my dad just stared at me as if he couldn't believe his ears. I knew that I was letting him down and letting the Lord down. My mother would never believe that I was a Christian after that. I ran from the house and I didn't go back until dad's funeral. It was too late to ask his forgiveness and it was too hard to ask mother's. I just couldn't. I was afraid of another quarrel. I wanted to leave her without any more trouble.'

Jill was upset but she tried to tell me the rest.

'When I took up teaching here in the south end, I didn't know what kind of school it was. I had looked forward to my new students.' Her voice broke. 'They're not students, they're hoodlums. I'm so shattered. They lie, and cheat, and steal everything. You should hear their language. It's gutter language. They show no respect for anyone; God least of all. When I'm trying to teach they delight in telling me how godless they are. I teach Religious Instruction. Imagine me trying to teach them that. They're wicked. They are so rude and uncontrollable that I can't tell them anything. They won't listen. I've tried everything. I've threatened them, told them I'd report them, but they know better. They know that I want to keep my job so much that the last thing I'll do is admit I can't control them.'

She stopped, wiped her eyes and waited a moment.

'I'm afraid of them, too. Some of the boys are as big as men. The other night as I was going home they grabbed me and jostled me around, just to scare me, I guess. They left bruises on my arms.'

Jill pulled off her cardigan. Big bluish-green splotches like smudged finger-prints were on her upper arms. I felt ashamed when I looked at them and recalled how I had hurried past her in the hall, wishing I didn't have to talk to her.

'My God,' I thought, 'how this poor girl is suffering. Not only are her arms bruised, she is deeply hurt within. Oh Lord, forgive me. Help me.'

As she pulled her cardigan on she said, 'I'm terrified. I actually tremble before I go into my classroom. I almost hate them. I have this dread of something terrible that might happen all the time. Even when I'm not there I'm nervous. I can't sleep at night. Yet, I'm so depressed when I come to college that I can hardly think . . . I keep going to sleep in class.'

She looked tired. She was trying hard to succeed, to outlive her mother's predictions of failure. She was fighting a hard battle all alone.

'Have you made any friends at your school among the staff, or here at college, Jill?'

'I don't have any close friends. I can't relate with anybody on the staff at school. I really don't want them to know about my problems. All the students here at college seem so happy and spiritual, I'm ashamed to let them know about my troubles. Besides, they would be really shocked if they knew how I acted with my mother and with my class.'

16

'All Christians have inner conflicts, Jill. They have them for the same reason that you have them. They are regenerated, born again, like you. When we are born again we become spiritual. Every Christian is spiritual by new birth, as he is physical by his natural birth. To be spiritual is to be regenerated, alive spiritually by the indwelling Holy Spirit. Spirituality is how you're living that spiritual life. The aliveness is dependent upon many factors and greatly differs in each person. Our families, our physical and emotional constitution, our environment, temperament, our calling and the purpose of God in our lives, all these determine our spirituality. Only God can truly evaluate whether we are living out our spirituality.'

Jill was quietly listening.

'Did you have a church home before you came here to London?' I asked.

'Oh yes. The friend that led me to Christ took me to her church. I had good teaching, plenty of spiritual food. The leadership in the church was strong. Everybody helped me and prayed for me when I was thinking about coming here. That's why I am so ashamed. It's not as if I didn't have a good start when I became a Christian. I should know better. There is no excuse for me to be so defeated.'

'But Jill,' I interrupted, 'I have found that the lack of spiritual food, fellowship or leadership is not the main factor in Christians failing to resolve their inner conflicts. Where these factors are present, it is a great help, but they are not essential. I've talked to people who had hardly any follow-up at all, yet they overcame and became strong Christians. They had one main essential.'

'What's that?' Jill asked.

'The desire to go on.'

'Oh, I do want to go on, to be an overcomer,' Jill insisted. 'When I started talking to you today I was ready to quit, but I don't really want to. I just don't know how to go on.'

'If the desire is there, Jill, there's nothing to stop you. God will help you, if you are willing to help your-self to his help.

'First of all, accept the Christian life as a life of conflict. Then, determine that you will allow those conflicts to change you for the better, not for the worse. You must say, "Yes, I've got problems, but my problems don't have me." '

Jill said it right then. 'I've got problems, but my problems don't have me.' She was beginning to look happier.

'Inner conflicts puzzle people,' I said. 'They get confused. They see the big gap between what the Bible says they should be and what they are, and they can't see any way to bridge it. So, they become either phonies, problems or prodigals. The phoney puts on a smiling face and says "I have no problems." The prodigal goes away and never tries any more. The others can't hide their problems and become obsessed by them and talk about them all the time.'

'Do you think that's what I am, a problem person?' Jill asked.

I quickly reached out towards her. Her question hurt me, for I knew I had been wrong when I had labelled her a problem person in my mind.

'Jill, I know that I acted that way. Please forgive me, I was wrong. I believe you are going to resolve your problems and become a conqueror.'

We prayed together and asked the Lord to help us both.

During the following weeks Jill began to develop

new attitudes and looked away from herself to the Lord. She confessed her doubts and declared God's truth. Instead of fearing difficulties she accepted them as doors to enter. She reached a better understanding of God, of her students, her mother and of herself. She was weak, but she was willing. What she wanted most of all was to go on.

We started by correcting her thinking about college. She accepted the fact that attending a Christian college, or church or anything like that, did not insulate her from problems. She began to realise that her commitment to the Lord guaranteed that she would be tested by God and tempted by the devil. Also, she had to see that the other students were not more spiritual than her; that becoming a Christian meant that she was still human, but it also meant that she had spiritual life enabling her to live a more abundantly human life.

When Jill realised these things she felt more tolerant with herself, and was prepared to be more open with her Christian friends. She shared her weaknesses and asked them to pray for her. Her motives for living for Christ and attending college changed from wanting to shed problems and escape threatening circumstances to wanting to learn how to live and love.

Together we worked back through her problems to find God's purposes for her in the school where she taught. She began to see her mistake of rejecting the class because they did not like her, nor agree with her. She confessed her rejection to God and asked for his love. Love released her from fear. She confessed that she was not adequate to cope by herself and asked others to help her. She attempted to accept her class as they were, not as she wanted them to be. She prayed that she would love them as they were, and admitted at the same time that she couldn't. God helped her and in time she was able to say some of these things to the class. Her new attitudes came out in her lessons. She began to laugh with them, with a genuine love coming through. She was saying to them by her actions, 'I accept you as you are. Even if you don't change, I'll stick with you. I believe that God's love in my heart is greater than the hate in yours.'

She and her friends at Christian Life College began to take authority and bind the devil that threatened her and affected the young people in her class. The powers of evil were bound; they proclaimed Jill free to teach and her students free to learn because of the presence of Christ in her. Miraculously the classroom atmosphere changed, slowly edging out the opposition.

Next, Jill realised the hostility in her heart towards her mother. Her hostility was expressed by her alienation. She had cut herself off from her mother. Her inner wounds were soreness in her soul. She remembered the hurts and didn't want to be hurt again. An independence had developed her self-defence against pain. She was afraid of losing that independence if she went back to see her mother. Would she lose her self-protection? Would she be humiliated, shamed and another severance take place? Yet the need for attachment, the need to be deeply healed, demanded reconciliation. That meant her independence was at stake. How could she be reconciled with her mother without losing her detachment; her standing alone position? To go back was to confess that she needed her mother. Finally, Jill confessed to herself that she was not standing but falling apart in her loneliness. In time, she was willing to go home. Her independence had been destructive. Her detachment from everyone who could relate to her was breaking her down piece by piece. All her conflicts were signs of her alienation and resistance to reconciliation. It was the hardest step back, but it was the most important. She worked her way back, with the prayers of her friends, to her mother. When they met she found her lonelier than she had ever known her. Her mother's jealousy was gone. They were ready for reconciliation.

Jill's problems proved to be avenues leading her to triumph.

2
What is the Overlap?

Helping Jill to help herself led me to an interesting and surprising discovery. I discovered the Overlap.

I discovered it while I was doodling. Jill was finding it difficult to understand why she was having so many problems since she had become a Christian. She had thought that her problems would decrease in number and complexity once she started to live for Christ. Instead she had found that while some disappeared, others evolved that were very hard for her to understand. The very nature of them seemed foreign to her. As I thought about her I drew two circles on my writing pad. Almost absentmindedly I scribbled in the right hand one, 'The biblical revelation'; in the left one, 'The human experience'.

'There!' I thought. 'On one side is the whole glorious revelation of God. That revelation is the Word, expressed in letter, in flesh and in spirit. In the other circle is man in this world, experiencing life and death.' I stared at the two circles. I wondered, on which side is Jill? Was she in 'the human experience' sphere or 'the biblical revelation' sphere? She was in both, I told myself. How could she be in both? Then, I drew two more circles that overlapped. Suddenly, there before my eyes, was a new sphere. 'Why,' I exclaimed, 'it's the Overlap; she is in the Overlap.'

What is the Overlap? It is the state of in-between. It

Biblical
Revelation
Human
Experience
Revelation

is the result of receiving the living Word, in letter, in spirit and in flesh within our human experience. The combination of divinity and humanity within the Overlap, in the in-between, produces the conflicts that emerge in the real life of the Christian.

The overlap of opposites, light upon darkness, truth opposing untruth, purpose clashing with no-purpose, the struggle of our will against God's will, produces the conflicts that bring about the changes in us. Change often causes confusion. The Christian sometimes does not recognise what is defeat or victory; he doesn't know who is conquering whom.

When a person becomes a Christian, the old is over and the new begins. What is over? Obviously the environment, one's world, is still the same. It is also apparent that a Christian remains human. His human experiences continue. The difference is that life without conscious contact with God is over, the old life, outside of the Overlap, is over. Human experience without the life of God has passed away. New life in the light of the biblical revelation changes one's conduct, viewpoint and attitude. Consequently everything becomes new within the Overlap. Often one doesn't realise that the old life style is not immediately changed by the new life within. While one is learning through the biblical revelation new things about the kingdom of God, one is also remembering things learned in one's past human experiences. The unforgettable past and the present new revelation create a learning experience that can only be described as conflict.

The Christian is a middle-man between the old and the new. Between the old life patterns and the new life goals is an exciting adventure called life in the Overlap.

The real life of the Christian is not what he was, nor what he will be, but what he is now. He should not live as though he were always almost there. He is very much *here*, where he really belongs.

After Jill came to Jesus she felt she had double trouble. She'd brought into the Overlap her world, her family, her job, herself. Jesus met her in the Overlap world, which included his family, his work, himself. Together they had a new life. It was an abundant life full of exciting adventures between the two, but not without conflict. The challenge was to get it all together; his family and her family, his work and her job, himself and herself.

What it amounted to was that the Overlap became the place to learn how to live in the kingdom of God as a child of God. It was not easy. It posed the problem of learning how to live with a king.

Life in the kingdom of God is hard because in one sense we are not in it. It is not as if we moved out of this world into the next, or from earth to heaven. We can't point to a palace in a capital city and declare that is where my king lives. We are not in the kingdom of God in that sense. In another way we are, for the kingdom of God is within us. So, while we are still in this world we are also under a new government and belong to another kingdom. Wherever we are, we are in the kingdom of God, for it is in us and has power over us. That is why we have conflicts after becoming Christians, for there is a power struggle between the two, the world we live in and the kingdom that lives in us. Answering to the authority of Jesus over all our human experiences in this world is the adventure of the real life in the Overlap. The proclamation of the kingdom and its embodiment in the person of him who is its King provokes conflicts that develop faith.

The kingdom of God is not only a message of Jesus but the person of Jesus himself. He causes decisive change. The life in the Overlap re-orientates the believer. It reverses his values and demands surrender of his own royalty.

The kingship of Jesus within us is the beginning of the new life and the ending of the old. The new morality that develops in us is governed by our perspective of the kingdom and our hope of when the kingdom of God will be completely over the whole world of people and things.

I discovered the Overlap by drawing with a pen on paper, but the real Overlap was not made by pen and paper but flesh and blood. The Word made flesh, drew the revelation into the human experience and created a new sphere of life for God and man. It is called the Incarnation. Before I tell you how that happened, let me tell you about Eric.

3
I'm not what I was

Eric stepped back into the shadows behind the tall shrubs. He was six foot and well built, with a dark, rugged handsomness. He kept out of sight, away from the crowd who casually walked along the waterfront. Hidden in the darkness of the park entrance he was able to see without being seen. He watched each approaching figure, and waited. A policeman crossed the street. Eric stood still, barely breathing. The uniformed figure stopped, stared into his dark corner, squinted and strolled on. Eric shivered and waited. He was cold and hungry and he didn't like being alone.

Then he saw him. The thin legs in stained levis were unmistakable. The hunched figure, hands in his jacket to keep warm and face hidden behind a thick beard under a mop of tangled hair, hobbled with an unmistakable limp over to the entrance of the park. He stopped, looked slowly around and then stepped into the shadows and hissed: 'Sss-sst, are ye there?'

'Yeah. I told ya I'd be here, didn't I?'

'Got the stuff?'

'Here.' A small packet passed between them, hand to hand. 'It's a good bag.'

'Here's the money, like we said.'

Eric turned to walk away. He didn't ask questions, he just passed the stuff on. This nameless contact meant nothing to him.

'If ya need a free cuppa coffee and a warm pad for a couple of hours, there's a place near the cemetery . . . a coffee bar. I was there last night. Bunch of weirdos run it . . . Christians.' The voice in the shadows spoke.

Eric groaned, 'Next to the fuzz, I hate Christians most. I don't need a cup of coffee that bad.' He walked away.

Eric didn't know exactly why he hated Christians. He had had little contact with them or the church, except for being christened as a baby and one wedding he'd been to. He didn't know if his mother ever went to church. She'd died when he was a little kid. His dad didn't go to church. When he was boarded out to a foster home after his mother died he hadn't had any religion.

Maybe he didn't like Christians because they were part of the establishment. He knew why he didn't like that. It wasn't long after his dad had remarried and he'd gone back to living with his new stepmother that he began to build up a rage against their generation. They stood for a middle-class, artificial life-style that he couldn't stand. While his folks fought and struggled to get more money to make more payments they didn't seem to notice him. They noticed how the world was falling apart around them, but didn't care. Nothing seemed to matter except themselves. To Eric their work and living were pointless and empty. Nothing made sense. The house was not a home, only a dormitory. The family weren't even friendly to one another, much less loved each other. Eric felt as if he was losing himself. He didn't matter to anybody. He lived with his parents but he felt like an orphan.

Then Eric found his brothers. Like the blossoming of the desert after spring rains, this new cultural climate created a rare joy for him. It was the joy of belonging. The alienated young in his town found each other and became the Flower People. They felt love and understanding for each other. They accepted each other as humans and it felt so good they called it Flower Power.

The establishment called them freaks and hippies. Eric put on a headband, let his hair grow and wore bells, flowers and beads. If they hadn't noticed him before, Eric's parents surely noticed him now. But the communication was not peace-making; it broadened the gap between them. Finally the ultimatum was pronounced. 'We have rules in this house. If you can't live under those rules, get out!' Eric got out. He was sixteen.

Eric was liberated. He was free to build his own values and life style. There would be no violence in his life against himself or anybody else. Nor would he get hung-up on elaborate plans for the future. He would live simply day by day. He wasn't going to shut anybody out nor hold anybody in; he'd just accept people as they were, not as he wanted them to be. He wouldn't ask anyone to change to be like him, nor would he change for anybody else. Each to his own.

As Eric turned his back to the glare of the neon lights along the waterfront to find a pad among the dark streets in the hills, he thought about the brothers he had lost.

When he dropped out of the establishment he went along with the Flower People in joyous abandonment to all the exhilaration of released feelings. He was free. He didn't feel hollow any more, but full of the excitement of discovering love. He felt like a poet. They lived near nature, started a commune, squatting in teepees that they erected with twelve-foot poles and a tarpaulin, building fires, watching the smoke curl up through the hole in the top to the stars. They experienced cold and heat, fasting and feasting, but never alone. Everything was opening out for them. With the help of pot and hash their consciousness expanded, until the expansion broke them up and carried them away, like faded blossoms blown across the fields. All the freshness, the beauty, the living together faded. They lost each other in the winds of change.

Within weeks Eric was wearing another costume, riding another beast and belonging to another brotherhood. He was one of the Devil's Disciples, leather jacket, motorbike and all. He had started on a bad trip down Disillusionment Road. The D.D.'s were a band of outlaw bikers. They roared around the country for kicks, indiscriminately sweeping on to village paths and whipping old ladies with bicycle chains. There were rumbles with Skinheads, and run-ins with the police.

'Yeah,' he thought, 'those were pretty wild times.' He remembered how he had broken his hand and got his face smashed in during a fight with some Skinheads. 'That's when I started dropping acid to get high. Trouble was I was stoned most of the time. I was out of touch. Couldn't ride my bike, had to sell it and my jacket, too.'

With no motorbike Eric was not much good to the Devil's Disciples. There was no need to hang on there, so he left. After all, that's why he'd dropped out of the rat race – home, school and job – so he could do his own thing. As for the jacket and the other stuff, he was glad to be rid of it. He felt more honest, somehow.

Eric couldn't find the address of the place he'd thought of going to so moved on to find a doorway, or any place out of the wind. Perhaps he should get back into town where he might find a discotheque.

It was the music that drew him into the hippie crowd after he'd left the Devil's Disciples. It penetrated his stupor and communicated better than words. He didn't listen much any more to what people said. The rock sound seemed to express how he felt deep inside. It said it for him. It screamed his screams. The hippie trip took him from dropping pills to shooting heroin. Living rough in squats, cars, bus stations and on the beach, he spaced out on drugs, soaring into an unseen, fantastic world, only to be shaken into half-consciousness by someone getting him out of the gutter. He took drugs to blow his mind, and he took them to get his head straight. It wasn't long before he began to work the streets in order to support the habit.

Working along the south coast he made contact with big liners, car ferries and pubs along the waterfront. He had to get money the best way he could, even though he'd got busted for possession of dope and fined. He was hooked.

Waking up one night in a squat, he discovered that his hippie friend had died of an accidental overdose. He ran into the street away from the corpse.

'God! He's the fifth friend to die so young. I'll never make it to twenty-one,' he thought, nor did he care.

Eric came down out of the hills back into town. He hurried towards the door of the discotheque. He reached inside his jacket where he had put his money. He'd better be careful. It was all he had, and his dole had been cut off. He hesitated.

For weeks he had been down. He was broke and he was lonely. Even a cup of coffee would help. He'd not forgotten about those weirdo Christians with their coffee bar. 'I guess I want a cup bad enough to even go there!' He turned towards the place across from the cemetery.

As he stood there in front of the house he felt close to something that he had wanted when he went with the Flower People. Maybe the wind would blow it back.

The coffee bar was in a house that looked just like anybody's house. There were no signs, no special lights, just a door bell. Eric was hungry so he went in. A girl in a long green dress stood near the door. She looked straight in his face and said, 'Hi!' and led him down a hallway to where the coffee was served. 'The music is up front there.' She motioned towards a dimly lit room. He took his coffee and several biscuits and made his way towards the music.

'Come in and sit where you like.' A guy in jeans and pullover stepped towards Eric. He was slim, blond and smiled a lot. Eric was prepared to be socked with religion, and this guy looked like the weirdo that would do it. He eased down to the low foam rubber square stool in the corner. He looked around and the guy was gone. He sat tense, but no one seemed to notice him much. He leaned back against the wall, sipped his coffee and let the music sink in.

The girl who met him at the door came into the room. She looked about twenty, with long brown hair and a friendly face. Everybody seemed to know her. She walked around with a plate of biscuits. Eric felt she was edging her way towards him. He braced himself for the questions he expected, like 'Do you know God?' or something like that. Frankly, he didn't know what to expect. This was not his scene.

'Any more?' She leaned over, offering him the biscuits. He took three. 'When you want more coffee, you know where it is.' She smiled. He liked the way she looked right at him. He smiled back. She moved on to the other side of the room.

'I'd better not hang around here too long or I'll get tipped off for sponging.' After a couple more cups, he left. No one had bothered him.

Eric went back spaced out the next time. The girl was there. She looked at him and he knew she realised how it was with him. She steered him into a corner, got him some coffee and went away.

'La Donna told me you were here.' It was the blond guy.

'La Donna, is that her name, the girl with the brown hair?'

'Yeah, her name is La Donna Darnall. She and another girl, Wendy, are usually around here.'

The next time he met Wendy. Norm, the blond guy, introduced them. She was tall and slim, the direct type. She came right to the point. 'Do you believe in God?' she asked.

Eric replied, 'There is no room in my mind for God at all.' Then he left.

A week later he returned. The free coffee and biscuits brought him back. Besides, he liked the informal crowd who were so friendly, even if he didn't know their God. He wasn't living anywhere and it was a roof for a little while. This time he let them talk about Jesus Christ and the Bible. They didn't throw it at him but they talked indirectly to the whole crowd. Sometimes they asked him what he thought about things. He and some of the other hippies threw in what they knew. One guy who had come in was in Divine Light, Buddhism and all kinds of things. He confused everybody with his philosophy. Eric didn't like his ideas, he wanted to hear more about the things these Christians knew. He was changing his mind about them being broomstick people, like witches.

When he heard others who looked and acted like

him and spoke his language, he listened to what they had to say. They talked about how they got their head straight after coming to God. They sang a lot and seemed to really love everybody. Eric began to ask his own questions; not aloud, but in his mind.

As he passed a church a few days later, he thought, 'There's people going into these places every week. They can't all be crazy. What is it that keeps them going?'

Everywhere he went the questions kept coming. While sitting in the park he looked at the trees and for the first time wondered about how they got there. The grass and flowers made him wonder if God had made this world. 'Perhaps God does exist,' he thought, and a shaft of light broke into his consciousness. As he walked away he knew he had begun to doubt what he had been standing for.

La Donna had said to Eric, 'When you give your heart to Jesus you'll understand a lot more about God and the Bible. It opens up your mind. God is real, Eric, and you can't just act like he is not around. That doesn't get rid of him. God is real and he loves you.'

Eric was alone in his bed-sitter when he tried out prayer. 'God, I don't believe in you. If you're around that's where I want to be. I want to give my life to you, but I'm not sure you're there. You are going to have to prove it. If you made this world, make yourself real to me.'

A soft wind blew through the place. Eric felt that knowing feeling. There were no bright lights, or fantastic visions like his psychedelic drugs gave him, but there was something. It was an instant, overwhelming impulse to go and tell the Christians at the coffee bar what he had done.

He told La Donna and let her share it with the rest.

Everybody got excited. He knew he wasn't exactly like them, but they were all sharing something together. As human beings they were all searching and finding what they all needed – love. They shared his moment, his experience, as if it was their own. They were really together, and somehow what hadn't meant much to him when he was alone meant everything to him now. They embraced and shouted and laughed together. Eric felt closer, warmer, more open to these people than he had felt before. They were a family.

The Flower People and the others had stuck together for survival, to protect each other from the law and the rest of society. They were held together by hate and rebellion. This new family was not hiding from anyone. They were open to God, each other and society. They were held together by love.

Everything began to happen. It was as if an invisible wall had been removed. He was close to God, to his new family and felt closer to the total environment, even to himself. They prayed with him, for he was open and told them his needs. He got a place to live. The government put him back on the dole until he was able to work. Love just seemed to come from everywhere. Eric got so excited about how prayer really worked that he asked God for all kinds of things. The practical things God supplied, the ridiculous, no.

Apparently God thought the guitar Eric asked for was necessary. Eric had accepted a small job for an elderly lady who needed some fixing-up done in her flat. He spotted a dusty guitar in the corner of a room almost as soon as he arrived. He wanted it so much. As he was leaving, she called him back, 'Here is a little gift for you.' She handed him the guitar.

Norman was the one who told Eric about the Baptist church nearby. 'They are going to have a baptismal service, Eric, and I'd like you to think about being baptised.'

'You mean, getting dunked?' Eric asked. He wasn't sure what it was for.

'Yes. Every Christian gets baptised to testify to his faith in God and that he believes in Jesus Christ as his Saviour.'

Eric hesitated. He knew that it would be a chopping off place for him. Once he took that step publicly in a church he was really into it. It would mean changing his ways and really living like a Christian.

'It's another experience, Eric, that takes you into a closer walk with the Lord. You identify,' Norman tried to explain, 'with Christ at his cross, his burial. That's what it means. You are buried with Christ. Then, when you come up out of the water, you are risen with him.'

The next Sunday the whole coffee bar gang were there, crowding the church to share Eric's baptism in water.

His eagerness to get back to making a living the right way led Eric in the wrong direction. He had the choice of going to a rehabilitation farm for former addicts or of taking a job redecorating a vicarage and living in a community. The tempting salary of thirty pounds a week looked far more appealing than the regulations and work on the farm. Although La Donna and the coffee bar family felt he should go to the farm he took the job in another town.

Although Eric was not quite so fiercely anti-establishment as he had been, he was not conditioned for the cultural shock he faced. The middle-class community, although Christian, wasn't able to accept Eric and another ex-junkie who had come to live and work among them. It was the Bowler Brigade versus the Revolutionaries. The young stared at the old, and the old at the young, in distress. They all fell into the generation gap. Eric and his friend left. They hitched to London. They couldn't stand the nine-to-five routine. On the streets of the city Eric found himself yearning to get back to his drugs, back into action.

One morning he awoke and told his friend, 'I'm going to my Christian friends down at the coffee bar. I don't believe they're like that Bowler Brigade we just left. All Christians are not tarred with the same brush. They are different.'

Things were different when he got back. Opposition had arisen to the coffee bar work. La Donna and Wendy had had to close down the work and all the gang were in a state of confusion. They tried to keep Eric involved but he began to look around. The Baptist church was too far away for him to go to. He needed a car to get there. Then there were other Christian groups but they were unapproachable socially. They didn't seem to see a person. Eric was up tight. Things were not working out as they did at first.

He got out his new, black, King James Bible. It was hard to understand. He couldn't get the guidance he needed as he had when they were all together. While the coffee bar was closing down and La Donna and Wendy were packing, Eric began to drift. He smoked a few joints and stared at the sky as he sat in a corner of the park. Maybe he would see things more clearly with a little help. He listened to his old music and the grass made him feel the sound. The day the coffee bar door shut and the crowd moved away, Eric got stoned.

Eric didn't drift very long, waiting for something to happen. He made it happen. He started mainlining and got into more trouble with the police. He revelled in the scene but he couldn't stop thinking about his Christian experience. One day a big group of his friends had a speed party. Gathered in a musty smelling, filthy flat they started to shoot the stuff, using each other's needles. After the ritual they began to feel good. Within weeks they were getting sick, so sick they couldn't stay in their dream world. One by one they went into the hospital. One died, others nearly died. If Eric had been mainlining longer he would never have survived. Hepatitis had ridden on that speed trip, straight into their blood streams.

When he felt strong enough, Eric headed for London. He knew that some of the coffee bar crowd were there. He had to find them. He had to find a way back to God. La Donna was in the United States, Norman had married and was working in the Baptist church and Wendy had married and gone to Cornwall. He found Nikki and Ena, old friends he'd met at the coffee bar. They were overjoyed to see him. He wasn't there long before they saw that he was really sick. 'You had better stay here with us. You can't live on the streets like you are.'

Nikki and Ena were attending Christian Life College. After the coffee bar folded up they decided they would try to get some training and teaching.

'You know, Eric, that is what you should do. You need to get back to God first. Then you could come to Christian Life College next term. I know La Donna would like that. Her dad is principal,' Ena said.

Nikki looked doubtful. 'I don't know if Elmer – that is what we call him – would let Eric in . . .'

Eric looked up. 'Why not?'

'Well, he is pretty strict about a person being stable and coming from a church with references from his pastor. It's a wonder we got in!'

'I'd like to see him,' Eric said. He felt challenged to prove that he could do it. Besides, he needed all the spiritual help he could get.

He went for an interview and left with some printed forms. Elmer told him about the evening classes in Christian service. He liked the idea.

Before he could make another appointment, he decided that he had better have a check-up at the hospital. He'd been sleeping with chicks and had V.D. Besides, he wasn't sure whether he really had hepatitis or not.

The next day the hospital phoned Nikki's flat. 'Is Eric there? If he is, get him over here at once. He's nearly dead on his feet. His liver is falling apart!'

Eric's spirits sank. Just when he was getting his life together again, and now this. 'Don't worry,' he told Ena and Nikki, 'I'll be back right away.'

Slowly he walked into a maze of corridors and asked for the ward. The porter looked at him, his eyes large with concern. 'Boy, everybody gets carried out of there feet first.'

Two weeks later they dismissed him from the hospital. He looked good and felt better than he had for a long time. Elmer said he could enrol for Christian Life College since his friends were there and he had nowhere else to go.

But it wasn't that easy.

Six weeks before the college term started Eric was on his way back to hospital. He told Elmer, 'I'll be out in time for college,' but Elmer thought to himself, 'more like time for Christmas.'

The students prayed for Eric. 'I'll go and see him again tomorrow,' Elmer said to them. I've got some cassettes for him to listen to. He's in isolation, you know. It gets pretty lonely for him.'

He found Eric feeling better and still talking about going to CLC. Eric then told him, 'They're going to do a liver biopsy on me.'

'A what?' Elmer was worried.

'The doctor came and told me how it would be done. They take this long hollow needle which makes a path for the next needle. With the second needle they're supposed to gradually pull out bits of liver that they need for the tests they want to make.'

'That sounds to me like a stab in the side that you'd get in a street fight!' said Elmer.

Elmer prayed that God would be with Eric.

Next day when Elmer arrived at the hospital, Pat, a student from CLC, was already there. Eric looked like death warmed up. Elmer and Pat stared, unable to believe the change they saw. It was hard to conceal their shock. He looked gaunt, his tall frame skin and bone. His dark eyes, like two burnt holes in a blanket, were glazed, showing up the fear within. Pain had drained him grey. His long, thick, wavy black hair seemed to be all that was left untouched by his awful sickness.

When he saw them he began to talk, as if he had been waiting to tell them what had happened.

Eric continued, 'Well, this Japanese lady doctor came with her needles. Step one was O.K. Everything went well. Then, step two. That's when everything went wrong. The instrument broke inside me. I looked down and part of it was sticking out of my side. They probed around trying to get the pieces out. All night long I was scared stiff. I thought part was left in me, but they got all the pieces out. Look,' he pushed back the sheet. His abdomen was swollen.

Elmer and Pat moved closer and took hold of Eric's hands.

'Eric, we are going to pray. God will take care of this.'

Eric remembered how he'd found his friend dead with an overdose two years before, and had looked at him and said, 'I'll never make it to twenty-one.' He was twenty now, and here he lay. He looked at Elmer. His dark eyes were troubled.

'I'll not get out of here.'

'Oh, yes, you will.' Elmer gripped his hand tighter. 'Let's pray.'

The three bowed their heads and turned to Jesus. Elmer thought he was going to die. He was deeply moved, desperate for Eric. They were in this together. Elmer knew God had a future for Eric. Gripping the hands of the two young men, Elmer spoke firmly: 'God, we've got to have a miracle. Jesus, you know what it is to be stabbed in the side.'

They left him in his small cubicle alone.

Eric went into a deep sleep. He hadn't really slept for days. In the morning when he woke he leaped out of bed, walked to the loo and was still walking around when the nurse found him.

'Hey, you, get back into that bed. You know you're not to go running around.'

Eric grinned, 'I feel good. I woke up with springs in my heels.'

When he was checked by the doctor his liver and spleen were normal size. His blood pressure was right. In a fortnight his blood count was down to normal. The doctor was flabbergasted.

Two weeks later, Eric walked out.

The thing he wanted most was to start at Christian Life College along with Nikki and Ena. He wondered if he would be able to. Physically he had a lot of re-building to do. Financially he was bust. Spiritually he was a bit better off, for he had been praying and reading his Bible in the hospital and had listened to teaching tapes. Yet he wasn't sure that he'd be able to make it for college.

Elmer sent a message. 'Come to the party for the new class.'

While Nikki and Ena were singing with a group, Elmer drew Eric aside. 'You've made it,' he said.

'Yeah, but I've not got the money. I don't think I can come.' Eric was worried about his fees.

'Oh, you've got to come. Someone has paid your first term's fees. With the help of your friends and your faith in God, you'll make it.'

A few months later Eric had a chance to tell everyone at chapel what God had done for him.

'It's fantastic. It blows my mind how it's all worked out. I've got a place to live, a job and my college fees are paid, even for next term. I'm learning to trust God's planning. I've learned you don't have to beg God for every little thing, like a pair of jeans. You trust him and he supplies. I've had my ups-and-downs. If anything unexpected happens it can still plunge me into depression, but I come out of it. For instance, I was almost bowled over by something that happened when I went home to see my folks during the school break. I no sooner started down the street when the police spotted me. They stood me up against a wall and searched me for drugs. Then they took me to the station. They were sure I was up to something.

'They asked: "We know you're living in London. What are you doing here?"

'They wouldn't believe it when I told them I was visiting my parents.

' "What're you doing in London?" they demanded.

‘ "Going to Christian Life College. I'm a Christian now."

‘ "What? That's a cover up . . . come off it!" ’

All the students in the chapel laughed.

One student exclaimed, 'It *is* a cover-up.'

4
How God got into the Overlap

When the student told Eric that it was a cover-up, he was explaining the cover-up in the Overlap. It was accomplished by a cross-over.

I talked one evening with a university student who was seeking salvation. After sharing a few verses of Scripture we prayed and she surrendered her life to Christ. Earnestly she asked him to forgive her and cleanse her from the sins that she confessed. Afterwards she looked at me, her face shining with joy. 'Why, I can hardly believe it has happened to me,' she exclaimed. 'It was so easy . . . unbelievably easy.' The symbol of the cross flashed into my mind. I said to her, 'It is easy for you and for me because he has done the hard part.'

The hard part was what brought about the cover-up in the Overlap. Within the biblical revelation we read that God faced a problem. Not his own, but ours: he was not taken by surprise but nevertheless it demanded his fullest grace and deepest love to solve it. It was the sin problem.

It started before and beyond Eden by one who knew good and evil. He was one of God's creatures with an angel's nature; yet he chose evil and became the unholy thing itself. Judged by his creator, Lucifer, the angel of light, became an exiled devil of darkness. As Satan, the adversary, and under the guise of a subtle,

Redemption

wild serpent-creature, he entered the garden where God had created man and woman. He urged them to question God's word. With hypnotic cunning he cast doubt on God's love. The venom of vengeance seethed in Satan's rebellious mind as he stung with his poisonous insinuations.

God had given to man a world to rule, a home to keep, and a woman who would share both with him. Most of all, God had given himself to them. His relationship with them developed their moral and spiritual faculties. He challenged them with responsibilities to their environment and to one another. To develop their trust in him, God gave them his words of commandment. Communion with God had to include recognition of divine authority. This would maintain the proper relationship between them. Obedience was to be the expression of man's respect and gratitude.

Before Satan came into the scene everything around man was God-approved. Also God had spelled out clearly what was not allowed. What God did not allow was evidently not good for man. In the day that they would eat of the tree of the knowledge of good and evil they would die.

Die? Did man understand the meaning of that word? Did man observe the death and decay in nature as the recycling of a balanced ecology? God did not ask for man's understanding of death, he asked for man's obedience to his Word; his trust in God's wisdom. Obedience would be man's expression of trust. His relationship was not to be based on coolheaded logic, but on warm-hearted love. He was challenged to retain a relationship, not to judge God's reasonableness.

Satan suggested that they would not die if they disobeyed God's word. They ate and immediately saw themselves exposed, bare of glory, disrobed of their innocence. Covering was sought. Foolishly they fumbled with fig leaves and finally fled, fearfully hiding among the trees. Gone was their purity. Lost was the beauty of holiness. Their noble dignity changed into the cringing, cowering conduct of the disobedient.

Inseparable in sinful shame, they hid from their holy God who came looking for them. He called, 'Where are you?' Where indeed! Here the severance began to painfully appear. Who was separated from whom? Not God from man, but man from God. Sin separated them. Who came, still seeking their fellowship? God! Man must have wished that God wouldn't bother to come again, but God came anyway. He would not let man conceal himself. He called him to give an account of his conduct. He insisted, as a loving Father would, that the transgression be confessed. Man and woman expected punishment for their disobedience, for they had been warned. It only remained for them to see what 'die' meant.

The human game of passing the buck started in the garden. Man blamed woman, and indirectly blamed God for giving her to him. The woman blamed the serpent and the buck stopped there. Although they had doubted God's word, the word remained. All were guilty and all were judged; the man, the woman and the serpent. Exile, increased sorrow, suffering and death would follow for man and woman. Man was spiritually dead and physically dying. The serpent was under the curse of God.

Sin-poisoned, man was under the sentence of death. The sin of disobedience had entered the blood stream and man was sinful. Disobedient by nature, he was a transgressor doomed to live in a cursed environment.

Hostility bristled, like thorns and thistles, within and without. He would wander, lost in this world. He would find no lasting rest, no peace. He had not lost his world but he had lost his special place in it. He had not lost his God but he had lost his special place with him. He was now a rebel at heart. Sin had separated him and alienated him from his God. He had become an enemy to his Father-Creator. He had lost his eternal life, his special life. He was eternally dead. This is what it meant to 'die'.

They were to leave the garden, separated from God, under the sentence of death, as prisoners to the penalty of sin. They would be slaves, sold to the power of sin. They could not leave their sin behind them. Sin was not a single act isolated from their persons. It was not an external deed. It was an internal disease. The poison that twisted their nature into a crippling sinfulness was in their veins. Separation from God's healthful holiness would speed up the processes of sin. Separation would turn into alienation with a furious speed, like a fever.

Was there no healing for the sin-sick pair? Did not God say something, do something to reveal mercy in the judgement he pronounced? Was there no covering to protect the exposed couple? Was there not a single sound of hope?

Yes! God said that Woman, of whom Satan took advantage in order to deceive man, would become the mother of a unique descendant who would inflict some kind of telling blow that would damage Satan's power to govern. The struggle would bruise that unique one's heel, but his weakness would be secondary to the damage his strength would cause to Satan. That promise was carefully veiled and it was a purposely oblique revelation of redemption: a plan which was already conceived in the eternal council of God. It would prove to be a revelation progressively developed before men and the devils. Mankind would understand it one day, for man was redeemable, but Satan, the unredeemable, would never understand it.

The promised unique one was hope for the future, but what of the present? God's Word was a lamp on the pathway ahead, but his love was a protective covering as they travelled towards their hope. Somewhere in the garden something was slain; blood was shed to provide a covering for the two sinners. God himself provided the sacrifice and supplied the covering. God made the skins into garments. He clothed them. He did not send them out without a covering. He put upon them garments made by his own design. He touched them as he dressed them. He could not let them go without comfort, some token, some covering; a final love-act before they went away. Those garments did not last for ever. They were made of the skins of animals and were temporary covering. These would wear out, more animals would be slain, and every time man needed a covering something had to die; blood had to be shed.

Sacrifice, blood, covering – all these are the elements of atonement. It could be that there, in Eden, man was asked to make an offering, by faith, with a lamb for forgiveness, even a temporary forgiveness, which was to be fortified again and again by repeated sacrifices. Altars appear in the very next chapter of human history, where the acceptable sacrifice was Abel's firstling of the flock. Adam's son with his offering was the first to say, 'Have faith. God has made a way for man to come back, forgiven. It is by the blood of the lamb.'

As sin increased in the human race, God's grace

extended beyond it. Sin deeply grieved the heart of God, but he had a plan. It was his family plan. It is the plan of redemption and comes through covenants that God established with individuals who built their altars and who offered the acceptable sacrifices.

Abel was the first. His offering was a first instalment on the final settlement for lasting reconciliation between man and God.

Noah shared more of God's plan with man. God made a covenant to save him and his family from the flood. Sin must be judged, but Noah found grace, or favour. By faith Noah obeyed God's word. He built his altar to the Lord and made a blood offering. God made his covenant with him unforgettable by setting a rainbow in the clouds. Through Noah God saved man and the earth from total destruction, but his plan of redemption was meant to go further than that. God planned a restored fellowship with mankind.

Abraham, another altar-building man, received more of God's plan through a covenant. Greater promises, which included the land of promise for his descendants, were given. Also included was the expression, 'I will be their God.' The holy, yearning love of God to have restored fellowship with man called out through that promise. Sin still stood in the way. God gave Abraham and his descendants a blood-token, the circumcision of every male. Abraham built his altars as God led him. Each time God revealed more of his plan. Eventually God asked Abraham to build an altar upon which he was to offer his son, Isaac. It was a supreme test of faith in the wisdom of God's command. To obey would seem to mean the destruction of the heir, through whom all the promises of God were to continue for future generations. When asked by Isaac, 'Where is the lamb for the burnt offering?' Abraham answered, 'God will himself provide the lamb for the burnt offering, my son.' At the moment of sacrifice God called, 'Abraham, Abraham.' God provided a ram in Isaac's stead. Through the covenant God made with Abraham a great family emerged, and they were called Israel.

God met another man on a mountain, one of the children of Israel, called Moses. He introduced himself to Moses as the immutable I AM, the God of Abraham, Isaac, and Jacob. He was determined to be identified as the God who kept covenant with man. He established his relationship with man. The children of Israel were swallowed up in the culture of Egypt by the time of Moses. They were slaves. Moses yearned for their deliverance. God revealed how they were to be delivered. It was more of the plan of redemption. Instructions were more explicit than in former covenants. They were to prepare for a journey. The head of each household was to take an unblemished lamb and kill it. The blood was to be sprinkled upon the door, top and sides, of each man's house. That same evening they were to eat of the roasted lamb with unleavened bread and bitter herbs. They were to stay inside, under the protection of the blood, until morning. That night a judgement would fall upon Egypt. The death angel would sweep through the darkness. The firstborn of each family would die, except in the homes where the blood of the lamb was applied. The blood would be a sign for deliverance, not only from death, but from slavery. That morning Pharaoh released all the men with their families to march towards Sinai. There God revealed his law and gave man more of his plan. A substitute was to be provided for man's forgiveness whenever he broke the law. An animal would be slain after the guilty offender laid his hand on the animal's head, confessing his sin. The man's guilt was transferred to the animal and God's judgement moved to the innocent substitute. The sacrifice upon the altar provided the means of forgiveness for the guilty through the intercession of the priesthood who administered the offering. This was called the atonement.

Upon altar after altar the sacrifices were repeated through the centuries. Prophets, priests and kings looked forwards to the perfect substitute, the eternal deliverer, the unique one. The prophetic voice grew distant and fell into four hundred years of silence. One day a vigorous voice was heard in the wilderness, 'Behold the Lamb of God, which taketh away the sin of the world.'

Here came Jesus. He started where God's voice left off in the past. He called everybody, the sinful, the sick, the fearful, the faithless, to come to him. Those who sat in the shadow of death lifted up their heads and listened. God was calling them. The poor heard the good news. Those enslaved by the devil were released. The blind received their sight. The oppressed were liberated. The broken-hearted realised that God loved them. The unique one had come.

He came not only with a message but with a ministry. He expressed it in word and in deed. He had come to establish a new covenant. The gradual revelation of God's plan of redemption was coming into full view. All the altars, all the ceremonies and covenants were to find their complete meaning in the new covenant established by Jesus. At the last supper with his disciples Jesus celebrated the passover. They remembered the deliverance their fathers had obtained by the blood of the lamb. Although the disciples may not have understood the meaning of his words, they were asked to take his body and blood through the bread and the wine as a new covenant for the forgiveness of sins. They were not required to understand but to trust the Saviour, as man was asked in the beginning to trust his creator. They were looking at the lamb. He was about to go to his altar, Calvary. The greatest day of atonement was dawning. Christ would have the sins of the world laid upon him, the guiltless for the guilty, the just for the unjust.

Sin would separate him from his Father, just as it had separated man. When he was made sin for sinners, their judgement fell upon him. That was his severest suffering. The anguish of separation from God is expressed in his bitter wail, 'My God, My God, why hast Thou forsaken me?' The Son of God became a substitutionary sacrifice, loaded with our sins. He had to die physically as a transgressor, and suffer the spiritual death of sinners – separation from God.

The last, longest and loudest cry on the cross, 'It is finished,' reached from eternity to eternity, from heaven to hell. It split the veil of the temple where the animal sacrifices were made by the priesthood of the old covenant and opened the new and living way. All the covenants, all the law, all the prophecies, all the plan was completed in him by his cross. The blood of Jesus satisfied the justice of God and opened the way to the throne of grace for every sinner. All can come boldly for help and have their past covered by Calvary: not only the past, but the present and the future.

How can we be sure? The proof of the full victory of the cross is declared by the angels, 'He is not here, he is risen.' The empty tomb is lasting evidence that Jesus' death was victorious over sin and the devil. Satan's legal, governmental and judicial claims upon the sons of man, children of disobedience, were no longer effective. His power was cancelled, annihilated. Christ's complete identification with sinners gave him the access to the very centre of Satan's strongholds in sheol. He died as one for all and was buried as one for all sinners. His soul was an offering for our sins, not his. He descended into the lower parts of the earth, or the underworld, and established his victory. He tasted spiritual, as well as physical death for every man. Into Satan's headship came sinlessness, bearing in his person the atonement for the sin of the world. He entered the dark and deep regions to release the righteous dead and transport them into the immediate presence of God. He snatched the keys of hell and death, and led the captives forth to share his exaltation at the Father's right hand. It was not possible for death to hold him. He spoiled principalities and powers, triumphing over them by his cross. He stripped the enemy, disarmed him. In his exaltation he sent the Spirit to say, 'Come, the blood of the lamb releases from guilt and slavery caused by sin. Come into the kingdom. It is the Father's pleasure to give it to you.'

That is what I meant when I said God has done the hard part. He has created the Overlap by sending his Son to us. Jesus is the biblical revelation in the human experience: the Word made flesh. His cross is the key to the kingdom of God. It is the way into the Overlap where you will be covered by the atonement. It is easy to be found when it is God who's seeking you.

5
I made it

'Don's gone again. He's been gone seven days. I've tried all the usual holes he falls into and he wasn't in any of them.'

Carol's voice wavered. She wasn't sure of herself.

'I don't know if I should ask you this or not . . .'

'You want me to help you find him, Carol?' It wasn't the first time she'd phoned me to ask for help to find Don. Her husband, a tall, lanky Texan was drunk more often than sober. At a certain point he would leave home and burrow into a wine cellar and stay there. Usually Carol would find him and bring him home to dry out.

Carol's voice rose, 'I don't know whether I should ask you to go with me, 'cause I don't know whether to go myself. I oughta just leave him where he is, wherever that is. Why bring him home? Little Donny and I are better off without him. Actually, we're happier when he's away. We have time for each other. When he's here all we do is think and talk about him; cleaning up his mess, arguing and fighting. I'm crying most of the time. Little Donny begs his daddy to stop drinking. The poor little kid keeps hoping, but I've lost hope.'

Little Donny was nine years old; a husky lad with a sensitive, compassionate nature. He loved both parents and had a sympathetic understanding of them that was surprising for his age.

'It's not right to ask you to leave your bed and come out at this time of the night...' Carol continued.

'Well, maybe for Donny's sake we should try, Carol.'

That seemed to remove the unreasonabless of looking for him, and she agreed.

At one o'clock in the morning we drove up in front of a dark hole of a place near the waterfront in a port city, miles from where they lived. We had been sent from one bar to another by those who claimed to have seen Don five days ago ... two days ... yesterday ... this morning. Had he staggered into this place? Somewhere he had to stop. A dirty red sign over the black doorway flickered, BAR OPEN. There were no windows. The night was starless. Everything around was shrouded in darkness. The doorway covered a hole in the ground, the entrance to a wine cellar, where souls could hide, out of sight, until their misery passed and they could face the light.

'I'll go in,' Carol said. 'No use you going into that hell hole if he's not there.'

She wearily lifted herself out of the car. Carol was a well-rounded, plump, good-looking woman. Her dark curly hair framed a cheerful face, with lively brown eyes. She was a sensitive person and it really didn't take much to make her smile or even laugh, in spite of the worry she had with Don. When she laughed, she laughed all over. Her whole body vibrated with joy. Her soft spot was Donny. She idolised him. He was the sunshine of her life. She lived to protect him from what his daddy was. Her eyes would get hard with rage when she talked about what Don had done to little Donny.

Don loved them both, but not more than his wine. He had not always been that way. Carol had told me how they met. He came to West Australia during

World War II. The US Navy were stationed at Fremantle for several months. He was drinking then, but he wasn't on wine. Carol thought he was having trouble handling the strong Aussie beer. She was sure that once he got out of the Navy he'd be O.K. She made excuses for him to her family. He was a likeable guy; tall, a slow grin that spread over his sun-tanned face, wrinkling around his blue eyes. He made Carol feel good when he'd come with chocolates and flowers, taking her out on dates to nice places. He was so thoughtful. He always wanted to know what she liked. She loved the way he talked with his soft Texan drawl. He could spin stories by the hour. He had a way of making her feel she was right there when he told a story. Sometimes Carol wondered if it happened exactly as he told it, but it didn't make much difference, just as long as he kept talking. By the time the ship was ready to leave they were head over heels in love. Don promised that he'd come back. Carol cried when he left. She wasn't sure if the tall Texan was telling the truth. But he did come back and he never left her, although he longed for Texas. He made West Australia his home, for Carol said she could never leave her family.

'It's a good thing I didn't,' she had said to me. 'If I'd gone over to Texas, what would've happened to me and little Donny when he turned into a drunkard?'

As I sat there waiting for Carol to come back through the black door, I wondered if Don would have become a wino back in Texas.

'He's here.' The door had opened and Carol's large figure filled the square of dim light. 'He's here. You'll have to help me. He is paralysed drunk.'

The hole was cluttered with chairs and tables, scattered around the bar and squeezed into dirty, dimly lit alcoves. There was hardly anyone around, except for a couple in a huddle and a witch of a woman behind the bar. She was old, a hag with red hair and a huge nose set in a florid face. Her eyes were small, ringed with mascara. Her red mouth was pinched, tight-set. She didn't say a word as Carol and I struggled with the passed-out Don. She had found him in a corner, slumped on the floor. The smell of stale wine and vomit that had dried on his jacket and trousers hit us as we tried to pull him to his feet. His swollen eyes opened a little, squinting out of his puffy red face. He was ashamed, but he was thankful.

'Oh, hello Carol . . . sorry . . . thanks for coming,' he wheezed as we pushed and pulled him towards the door.

Over the bar-room floor we dragged him, up the stone steps, out of the black door. After it closed we leaned against it. We were all out of breath. Don was heavy, his six-foot frame slumped between us, his arms around our shoulders. His feet dragged across the pavement as we pulled him to the car. I opened the door and we shoved him into the back seat. He gave a snort and began to snore.

As we drove home towards Perth, Carol was quiet, deep in thought. 'What are you thinking about?' I asked.

'I was remembering the day we walked into Victoria Park Town Hall. Don and I were already working on a divorce. A friend, one of the very few we still had, came over to see if he could help. He had seen the ads in the newspaper about your meetings.

' "Don" he said, "Some Americans are having services in the Town Hall. Why don't you go over there and ask them to help you. Maybe you could talk to one of your own countrymen better. I hear there have been some miracles through their prayers. It might help."

'You know I really felt like we should go when he told us about your meetings. We sure needed a miracle. But Don wasn't willing.

' "I know the tricks of those American evangelists. We have lots of them in Texas. They talk a lot, but nobody could live the way they tell you to. They try to get everybody on their knees, confessing their sins and all that!" He tried to laugh about it, but our friend said, "Well, a little down-on-your-knees stuff wouldn't hurt you, old boy." '

Carol went on talking about how they came, for some reason, on a Sunday morning. It was a communion service. Elmer preached. He knew that there were lots of new people there from different churches, and some from no church at all. He had told everyone that no matter what church they belonged to, if they loved Jesus they were welcome to share the bread and wine with us.

'I remember how he said, "If you don't know the Lord, but you need him, there is no better time than right now to kneel down and say with the rest of us that you accept the blood of Jesus for the forgiveness of your sins. We are all going to kneel at our seats. When we kneel, you kneel, too. If you want the Lord to help you, ask him. Say, Lord, I thank you for shedding your blood on the cross for me. I ask you to forgive my sins. I accept you as my Saviour who forgives all my sins."

'Don nudged me when he heard him say that. "I told you they'd get us on our knees." '

'Yes,' I interrupted Carol. 'I remember that, for I was sitting near you. As Elmer and the elders served the communion I slipped over to kneel beside you. I asked you if you knew the Lord or were you seeking him? You broke down and cried and told me how you needed him. Don was crying, too. He began to tell me about his drinking.'

'Well, it was a wonderful morning,' Carol said. She turned towards me and looked over her shoulder at the snoring, stinking figure in the back seat. 'Do you think there is any hope?'

Carol shook her head as if to answer her own question. 'Look at him. He's tried so hard to live it, but he just doesn't seem able to. I just let him out of my sight and he meets one of his old pals and is off again. You know, the day after we went to church and accepted the Lord, he went and told his friends what the Lord had done for him. He told them he was never going to drink again. Some of them wished him luck and others told him it wouldn't last, and it didn't. Now they just laugh at him and tell him he is just like them, no-hopers. What do you think?'

I tried to answer, but words didn't come easily. I was dead tired and feeling sick. The stench of that wine cellar and the sight of Don, bloated, filthy and passed-out in the back seat was not very encouraging. Yet, I didn't want to let Carol know how I felt.

'Oh, we never give up, Carol. Someday there will be the last time and Don will come through. Where there's life, there's hope.' I tried to look cheerful. Then, to make it sound more spiritual, 'With God all things are possible.'

Carol didn't say anything. We turned the corner and there was their house.

We got Don on to the mattress. There wasn't any bed, just a mattress on a frame. The whole house was nearly empty. Don and Carol, before the drink took over, had built and furnished a beautiful home. The house was red brick, with a terracotta tile roof. Don was a good builder and had designed a sprawled out ranch style home that stood out in contrast to the rest of the houses around. It was spacious on a large site that Carol's family had given them. As Don began to drink more and more he lost job after job. Finally he began to sell the furniture, not for food, but for wine. Carol worked hard to make the payments on their mortgage, while Don would carry the furniture out, piece by piece, until there was hardly a thing left.

'We wouldn't have a table to eat at if it wasn't that we built it in the breakfast nook. Thank God he can't sell that without tearing the house down. And it is a good thing I insisted that we put the whole place in my name, instead of his. We'd have lost it all by now.'

Don lay there, snoring in a stupor, while Carol and I sat on orange crates sipping coffee. I glanced around the empty room and at Don on his mattress. I touched the glistening walls.

'These are beautiful, Carol,' moving my fingers over the plastered surface. 'They look like mother of pearl. The texture is so unusual, like the inside of a sea shell.'

'Don did that. He's good at anything that has to do with building. But wine has burnt him out,' Carol said, glancing at the shell of a man on the mattress.

Don's eyes blinked. He rubbed them, giving a snort. Saliva ran out of his mouth over his unshaven chin. He turned his head to see who was standing beside him. Carol was on one side, I on the other.

He grinned at Carol. She reached out and took his hand. He looked at me and frowned. 'You here again?'

'Yes, I'm here again.'

'Well, go away. I don't wancha 'ere.' His speech was slurred. 'Go away. You're too good to be here. Don't touch me. I'm not fit for ya to touch. I'm filthy. Go away. I don't wancha 'ere.'

The weariness of the whole ordeal, the disgust I felt in my soul, the objections in my mind about the way he treated his wife and son . . . all of it rose up in me. I resented all of it . . . the sight of him, the smell of him, the sound of him.

'You're right, Don. You don't deserve my help, nor do you deserve your good wife and son. They're too good for you. You've used up Carol's life and you're wrecking Donny's. They love you and have given you every chance to straighten up. We've all prayed for you. Jesus has given you a chance, but you've thrown it all away for nothing. I'm leaving. I don't have to stay, but I'm sorry for Carol.'

I turned to leave. I didn't look at Carol. I walked straight for the bedroom door. I reached for the door knob. I couldn't turn it. I was caught in a stream of divine love, as if I was under a magnetic power. An invisible force held me. I couldn't leave. There was no way to move, except to turn around and walk back to Don. I stood by his mattress. His bleary eyes were wide open, a little frightened. He didn't know what to expect.

'You're right, Don. You don't deserve my help. You don't deserve the love of your wife and boy. You don't deserve God's love, but that doesn't change the fact that he loves you. He just keeps on loving you.'

I was crying and so was Carol.

'Don, God loves you and he is going to make you a fisher of men!'

Don raised himself on one elbow. He shook his head and looked at me. His eyes could hardly focus. 'Wotcha say?' he slurred.

62

'I said, God loves you and he is going to make you a fisher of men.'

He slowly sat up. He tried to get up. Carol helped him. Finally he stood. He wobbled, swayed and tried to look straight into my eyes, peering, leaning towards me.

'Did ya say that God's gonna make me a fisher of men?'

'Yes.'

'All right. If ya say God's gonna make me a fisher of men, I'll be a fisher of men!'

I stared at him. He stared back. Carol seemed to be holding her breath. None of us said a word. It seemed a long silence, as if we were waiting for the words he had just spoken to reach heaven or hell or somewhere. We knew they were powerful. They were going to change his life.

Suddenly I reached up and took his puffy face firmly in my hands. I looked into his eyes.

'In the name of Jesus, I command the evil spirits that have oppressed this man to leave. By the power of the Holy Spirit he will be what God's love will make him be ... a fisher of men. By faith in the blood of Jesus I proclaim deliverance for you, Don.'

I stepped back. A slight shudder seemed to roll down through him from head to toe. He covered his face with his hands and wept. When he looked up, the slow grin spread over his face and his eyes shone with hope.

I sang as I drove home through the dark streets of Perth at three o'clock that morning.

The next week I was invited to a birthday party for little Donny. As we sat in the breakfast nook, Donny was about to blow out the candles on his cake. 'Make a wish, Donny,' I urged.

'Can't,' he said. 'My biggest wish has come true. Daddy's here.'

Don reached over and gave the boy a hug. His face glowed with joy. Carol wiped tears from her face. Donny looked at me. 'Know what? I'm ten years old today and this is the first time I can remember that my daddy was at my birthday party.'

It wasn't all victory for Don. Change never is easy. The war was won. He was free from the bondage, but he was not free from the temptation. Old friends still stopped him, inviting him for a drink. He was selling retread tyres. Every time he made a sale a drink was suggested. Most of the time he resisted, sometimes he accepted. But he didn't run away any more. No more dropping out of sight for days. He came home and he and Carol would get mad at each other, and then pray and make up. We prayed, too. Elmer and I did all we could to encourage him.

I tried to show him that he was in a different position than before. 'Don't give up, Don. This is just the mopping up exercise. Like when the navy took over a beachhead during the war. They had to go on and drive the enemy out of every inch of ground they had taken over. You're on the victory side. You've got the enemy on the run.'

Elmer got alongside to help him too. 'Don, we're going to have a baptismal service next week. I want you to be there. You promised to get baptised before you landed up in that wine cellar in Freemantle.' Don hesitated. 'I don't know. I'm not sure if I should. What if I fail and let you down?'

'Sure, you're liable to fail and let us down, Don. We're all liable to fail and let each other down. But the Lord isn't going to fail. He won't let any of us down. We're going to trust him together, Don.'

On the day of the baptismal service the phone rang. 'It's Don,' Carol said. 'He's late coming home. He should have been here an hour ago. He went to sell some tyres to somebody. You'd better pray or he'll not be back in time to get ready for the service. If he doesn't get back, I can't come, nor Donny. We all want to be baptised.'

'We'll pray.' An SOS went out to the church family. 'Pray for Don.'

The local pastor of a Baptist church had happily lent us their baptistry for the new converts from our meetings in the Town Hall. Elmer was anxiously waiting at the church door.

It was nearly time for the baptismal service. Don and Carol were not there. Elmer took one more look up the street. He lifted his arm and waved. 'There they are! Praise the Lord, here comes Don!'

When Don stood in the water beside Elmer, he grinned. 'I made it.'

'Yes, thank God, you made it. Don, I believe that as you take this step of obedience God will help you to be an overcomer.'

Elmer was right. God did help Don, and he never drank again. Later he started a church in the very neighbourhood in which he had staggered as a wino. He became, and still is, by the love of God, a fisher of men.

6
How do we get into the Overlap?

Don was in the Overlap. He was in the kingdom of God. Love had lifted him to his feet and he stood weak, wobbly, bleary-eyed, but he stood, in the kingdom of God.

How does anyone get into the Overlap? It's hard to understand how a slave of sin can become a son of God; a guilty prisoner cleared of all guilt. Shall we point to the cross? Is that the place and the power? Or shall we declare that the throne of God is where the guilty are set free and the slave becomes an heir? It must be there through the advocacy of the risen Christ that freedom is given within the vast limits of the kingdom of God. But the cross and the throne are a partial answer to the question of how to get into the Overlap. They are one-sided, God's side. Redemption and the consequent exaltation of Jesus Christ is how God got into the Overlap. In fact, that is how the Overlap originated. He brought the biblical revelation into our human experience by his life and brought the human experience into the biblical revelation by his death and resurrection. The power of redemption, and all the subsequent upheavals that shook hell, broke open the grave, split the invisible dimension that barricaded the dead from his presence and elevated him and those whom he took with him to the Father's right hand, that power is in the Overlap.

Regeneration

Those were the steps God took, incarnation, redemption, resurrection, exaltation. They were the
steps that caused radical change in heaven, hell and on
earth. What are the steps that we must take that will
cause radical change in us?

Getting into the Overlap is a little difficult because
we are spiritually in the dark. In fact our darkness is a
blindness caused by no light. Like a deep sea fish
which has not developed its faculties for seeing, we
prefer darkness to light. There has to be a radical
change within caused by some external power before
we can possibly approach and enter the kingdom
of God. That is why unchanged people attempt
to enter and retreat into their darkness. Without
a creative change they cannot tolerate the light
in the Overlap. They cannot live in it. The change
that is required is regeneration within their deepest
selves.

The first step towards that change is spiritual revelation. Without it one cannot see, much less live in the
kingdom of God. One cannot reveal it to oneself. A
revealer has been sent into our world to lead seekers,
much like a guide would lead the blind. He, the Holy
Spirit, has been sent by the Father in the name of the
Son, to reveal, to teach and to convince each person of
the reality of life in the Overlap.

He attracts a person to Jesus. Then, he begins to
convince him that he needs Jesus. One can sense the
light outside of the Overlap, and still not be a believer.
Saying 'I see the light,' is not being in it. Coming
towards the light is not yet the encounter that opens
one's understanding into a tranforming, believing experience. Seeing the light, or rather sensing its presence, is like a blind man feeling the presence of a
person, or noticing an interesting change of shadows

in his darkness. Until he is touched by the light he keeps asking 'Who is it?'

When one responds to the revelation of Jesus one may confess that Jesus is the Son of God, but such a confession does not necessarily save one. It is the first step towards the confession that will. It is much easier to give assent to the deity of Jesus Christ, than it is to give him the right to save me. Giving God that right demands one's confession as a sinner who needs Jesus Christ to save one from one's sins. Both confessions, the confession of Jesus as the Son of God and the confession of our sinful selves needing him as our only Saviour, spring from the revelation given to us by the Holy Spirit. He presses into some by a steady dawning and he bursts into others by a sudden illuminating blast-happening. Sometimes both. He silently pursues us in the dark, and then suddenly turns on the light and shouts, 'Look, look at the lamb of God.'

When our hearts respond to the revelation of the Son as Saviour of our sinful selves, we are born into that which has been revealed. We move into the Overlap. Revelation draws us to regeneration.

We don't come to know the Son by standing back and appraising him as a collector would at an auction. Knowing Christ is not a detached, impersonal learning process. It is an encounter, an experience that may include, but must go beyond an objective, intellectual approach.

Loyalty to one's former choices and decisions often hinders venturing into the new life within the Overlap. If those decisions and choices have been made for one's own good, then loyalty to them may help one to enter in. If not, one may find it hard to accept the conflicts that regeneration can produce. Changing sides is often an admission that one has made wrong choices and can't see any hope in the way one is going. It is hard, for one wants to continue thinking one is right, even when wrong. To hold back is to remain hidden in darkness. Like sheep, one goes astray and keeps turning to one's own way. As a small boy, lost in a department store, sobbed, 'I kept getting loster all the time.'

Why are those outside the Overlap lost and losing? They are separated from the power that could give them spiritual sight and life. Their choices have kept them from God. No one need remain outside, for God has come to show each person the way into the real life.

Sometimes it is not loyalty to one's choices, right or wrong, that keeps one from coming into the new life. It can be partial confession. A seeker can insist that he believes that Jesus is the Son of God and still be in the dark. Saying so does not always indicate that one understands the statement. I'm sure I didn't the first time I said it, nor the second time either. Whether it is understood by us or not, it can be understood by the enemy of our souls. Satan makes it even more difficult for them to find God.

To say that Jesus is the Son of God means that Jesus existed before he was born at Bethlehem. It means he is God, eternal and immutable. It means that when he was born he was born as God in this world, but with all the involvement of pregnancy and travail, the water, blood and crying, like you and I. The difference was the conception. He was conceived by the Holy Ghost. Can a man say that he really believes this, unless the Holy Spirit has revealed Jesus Christ as Saviour to him? Why do men without the revelation of the Holy Spirit, say they believe Jesus Christ is the Son of God? Fear? Are they afraid of not believing and thereby missing salvation? Or is it pride? Is there a pride of being able to claim something so mystical, so inexplicable, that feeds the ego of man? Does it make one feel spiritually superior to say that one believes that Jesus Christ is the Son of God? Or is it an effort to build up a relationship with a deity that seems to want one's affection and needs one's loyalty? Any of these are more emotional than intellectual, and either way they are self-centred and move a person further from the cross rather than closer to it. They do not lead to repentance.

Revelation that leads to repentance results in regeneration. The regenerated man who believes that Jesus is the Son of God, believes in the virgin birth and the pre-existence of the Son, and much more. He believes what Jesus taught while he was on earth. He believes the New Testament record is authentic and authoritative. He accepts and believes God's Word, even when not fully understood. He accepts the miracles, the life, death and resurrection record. The regenerated man believes that the cross is not a tragedy but a triumph. His believing is a statement of faith, not a rational argument. He insists upon believing because he is convinced that Jesus Christ is not only the Son of God, but his only Saviour. He knows it and even if he doesn't know all the implications, he says so, because he believes it is so. He stakes his salvation on it, and it works.

During the Jesus Revolution many youths came out of the darkness of the counter-culture exclaiming, 'Turned on man. We're turned on.' They were regenerated, the light was on. They were born again and consequently they were in the light and they were seeing life as they never saw it before.

Regeneration is not getting into the light, it is the

light getting into us. Jesus, the light, comes and brings his life with him into us. The regenerated man is not merely a man re-made. He is a man changed by the unchangeable Christ. He has Christ's life within producing a new life-style. He has a new life source. It is Christ's indwelling presence which enables him to live according to the will of God. Regeneration will produce new problems, but in the new nature there is power to resolve conflicts turning them into lasting victories.

What 'turned on' when Don was regenerated, or when the Jesus People believed? Outside the Overlap we live in a human experience sphere as body and soul people. We are partially alive. Spiritually, we are dead. As dead as a burnt out lamp. A dead bulb is recognisable as a light bulb. The filament and the outward glass form show its potential, but there is no illumination, for there is no power. When we live without God, there is no spiritual power. Our souls show our potential. Our bodies identify our existence as human. The deadness of our spirit leaves us and others around us in the dark as to our real purpose. We are merely human, ornamental, within our world. We are not relating to God, nor to his world, as his children.

What is this power that turns people on, and transports them from a mere human experience in spiritual darkness into a new life? What transforms them? How does the brilliance of the biblical revelation become an actual new life, something real and dazzling, alive? It is the power of the Holy Spirit. It is his power that changes us. It is his power that causes us to have conflicts and enables us to conquer those conflicts. He changes us into body, soul and spirit people. Correction. He changes us into spirit, soul and body people. He turns us up-side-down and that means that

72

we get really shaken and surprised at some of the things that fall out. A young person said to me, 'Living with the Holy Spirit isn't easy, but after you've agreed to it, there's no other way to live. There's just nothing else like it. It's great.'

So Jesus comes to us within our human experience and he reveals to us his love. We see the kingdom and we long for it. But we can never get into it until we are born again. We cannot transport ourselves from the human experience into the Overlap, any more than we can take ourselves from earth to heaven. We must be born again, regenerated. That means letting Christ come into us. It is not merely a childish Sunday school lyric, 'Into my heart, Into my heart, Come into my heart Lord Jesus.' It is the sinner's prayer at any age, for unless we become as little children, we shall in no wise enter the kingdom.

Once in, you are a new you. New birth is a new creation. It is a transportation from one sphere of living to another, from the old to the new, from slavery to freedom. It is an exodus from the body-soul existence of the human experience, into the spirit, soul and body biblical experience within. Once we were blind, but now we can see; lost, now we are found. It's like getting a new heart, or a new control centre. Instead of only reacting to wordly stimuli, we are, by the Spirit's life in us, able to live and act decisively and willingly according to his inner stimulus. Our new control centre is in the spirit, rather than in the soul. We have an alternative to the demands of the flesh. It is the promptings of the Holy Spirit who tells us what will glorify Jesus and please God. God, through regeneration, has given to every Christian an indwelling presence that enables him to live according to the will of God. The indwelling presence produces a new life force within that proceeds to change our lives.

Once we walked as the living dead. Spiritual death separated us from God. We were cut off from the power source for eternal life. Instead we had eternal death. Now, through regeneration we are no longer without God. The deeds we did under the judgement of death are all forgiven and our guilt removed. United to God, we are made right in his sight, through Jesus Christ. We are acquitted. He justifies us to right standing, by his holiness. Regeneration has taken us from the slave market to the throne room; from the law court where we stood guilty before our judge, to the right hand of God, where we stand before our Saviour.

7
Stiff with fear

The sudden insistent buzz of the phone broke the thread of Elmer's thoughts. With frayed nerves he answered, 'Yes?'

'Sorry to disturb you, but it's Dr Harkins on the phone and I thought you'd want to talk to him. Sounds urgent.'

'Thanks, Rosemary, put him on.'

The doctor's amiable voice sounded concerned. 'Elmer, I would appreciate a little help with a patient of mine. He's agreed to me asking you.'

'If I can, I'd be glad to. What's the problem?'

Elmer knew that Dr Harkins wouldn't be asking without due consideration. Both men were extremely busy – Elmer with the college and the doctor with his surgery and hospital duty. Dr Harkins also gave much of his own time to teach at Christian Life College.

'He's a Christian, but so deeply affected with fear that he is practically paralysed, emotionally and mentally. At times he can't even move physically. I think his problem is more spiritual than physical. There is little I can do medically.'

'What are you suggesting?'

'Could we meet at his home tonight?'

Elmer agreed. That evening he met Fred. The man was slight of build, but it was difficult to say whether he was a small man or not. Everything about him was diminishing: his posture slumped, with drooping shoulders and limp slack arms; his countenance, every muscle drawing every feature downwards into a wretched, miserable expression. His age was disguised so well by his expression that Elmer could only guess that Fred was perhaps pushing forty. It was hard to say which way.

Dr Harkins spoke softly, drawing Fred out of his slough of despondency word by word, sentence by sentence, until they were able to see some of the suffering he had within.

He was a hurt man who was still hurting with the fear of being hurt. True or not, he was sure that everything was aimed at hurting and humiliating him. His fear was so intense he could almost taste it. It was like a rope tying him up: he could feel it. He was alone, unwanted, misunderstood, and there was no help for him. He was terrified with loneliness. At times he couldn't talk or think. Sometimes he couldn't move.

'I am so fearful, I'm petrified. I can't get out of bed. I'm afraid to venture out.' Fred spoke slowly and so softly that it was more like a whisper than a voice.

He was worried about his job. 'I can't cope much longer with my class. I'm afraid of my students. They know I'm afraid and they take advantage of me. They ridicule me and even strike me, and I don't hit back, not even verbally. I just coil up inside. The class is a shambles. The worse they act, the worse I suffer. I dread going in each day.'

Anxiety had Fred feeling as if he was himself a catastrophy. He was overwhelmed. He was helpless to avert the trouble he was to himself or to others. He was inexorably withdrawing a little more each day, slowly petrifying.

'Fred, I'll tell you what we are going to do,' Elmer

76

said, glancing towards Dr Harkins. The doctor nodded in agreement, thankful for Elmer's direction.

Elmer reached for his Bible. 'We are going to look at some scriptures. You are weakened by your ordeal and the devil is attacking you. He is an enemy to us all and knows our weak spots. He strikes where we are vulnerable. Your anxiety has given the enemy an opening in your mind and he is attacking you with fear. We are going to overcome that enemy the same way Jesus resisted the devil in the wilderness. Jesus used the written Word of God. Satan knew the Word but Jesus knew it better. He not only knew the letter of it, but the spirit of it. He unsheathed the sword of the Spirit and declared, IT IS WRITTEN. Let's follow his example and use the Word of God.'

Elmer and Dr Harkins drew up closer to Fred so that he could look at the Scriptures with them. Elmer knew that Fred's mind was shrouded with darkness by the enemy's deception. It would be hard for him to even take it in, but the unfolding of the Word would give light; it would impart understanding. (Ps. 119: 130)

'Look, Fred,' Elmer pointed to the verse for him to read, 'it says, "Take the sword of the Spirit, which is the Word of God." (Eph. 6: 17) We are not defenceless. We are going to use that Word to resist the devil.'

Fred glanced apprehensively at Elmer, as if he was not quite ready to take on his opponent.

Dr Harkins reassured him. 'We are going to do it together, Fred. We are here to help you. God will give us active faith in his Word.' Elmer had found another scripture. 'Look at this,' again drawing Fred's eyes to the Scriptures. 'Resist the devil and he will flee from you.' (Jas. 4: 7)

Fred stared. He didn't have the will to exist, much less to resist.

'How will I do that?' he mumbled.

'By faith, Fred; like Dr Harkins said, God will give us faith – active faith.'

Elmer flipped over a few pages. 'Look, it reads "Resist him, firm in your faith." ' (1 Pet. 5: 8) Elmer leaned back, laid the Bible down, took a deep breath and smiled. 'So . . . now the next thing we are going to do is pray. We're going to ask God to help us to look up some scriptures that will especially help you, Fred. I'm sure God has something to say to you that will give you faith for your victory.'

They prayed and thanked God for his Word. They asked the Holy Spirit to guide them. They recognised the Word as the Sword of the Spirit. They knew that when the Holy Spirit quickened the Word it would be active and sharper than any two-edged sword, piercing to the division of the soul and the spirit, of joints and marrow, and discerning the thoughts and intentions of the heart. (Heb. 4: 12) The Word would get right to the heart of the trouble and unseat the enemy and set Fred free.

As Elmer picked up the Bible he knew that Fred's enemy was fear and the ground upon which he was being attacked was his anxiety.

'Fred, let's see what God has to say to us about fear.'

Holding the Word so that Fred had to look at it, Elmer read aloud:

'The Lord is my light and my salvation; whom shall I fear? The Lord is the stronghold of my life; of whom shall I be afraid?' (Ps. 27: 1)

'I guess I'm afraid of everything,' Fred moaned, as if to answer the question.

'That's what your fear says, Fred, but our faith says this!' He thumped the text with his finger. 'Look at it. Read it aloud.'

Ever so slowly Fred focused his eyes, forced his voice and read, 'The Lord is my light and my salvation; whom shall I fear? The Lord is the stronghold of my life; of whom shall I be afraid?' (Ps. 27: 1)

Dr Harkins said gently, 'Fred, it's not an interrogation, it is a proclamation.'

Elmer had found another scripture. 'Look at this.' All three read, 'Out of my distress I called on the Lord; the Lord answered me and set me free. With the Lord on my side I do not fear. What can man do to me?' (Ps. 118: 5–6)

'Another proclamation.' The doctor smiled.

'Talk about proclamations, listen to this one from St Paul: "What then shall we say to this? If God is for us, who is against us?" ' (Rom. 8: 31)

Dr Harkins added, 'What about that wonderful statement in 2 Timothy: "For God did not give us a spirit of timidity but a spirit of power and love and self-control."? ' (2 Tim. 1: 7)

Elmer said, 'Fred, the Holy Spirit has helped us to find selected scriptures for your personal use. I want to write these out for you, like a scriptual prescription.' Elmer looked around for some paper.

'I'll do that,' Dr Harkins said. 'Those are the kind of prescriptions I enjoy writing the most.'

'Fred,' Elmer handed him the scriptures, 'I want you to use these three times a day, like a tonic. The Word of God has life and active power in it. It works in the soul, the spirit and the body. (Prov. 4: 22) It ministers to the heart. It's good medicine for the whole man. You don't need to understand how it works, any more than you would need to understand everything about the medicine Dr Harkins would prescribe from the chemist. Just take these scriptures and let them work within you. It will strengthen you like good food, even more so. (Eph. 3: 20) Jesus quoted the Word to Satan and said, "It is written, Man shall not live by bread alone, but by every word that proceeds from the mouth of God." ' (Matt. 4: 4; Deut. 8: 3)

Fred took the prescription that Dr Harkins gave him. He read the scriptures and then looked up at Elmer. 'Did you say three times a day?'

'Yes, Fred,' Elmer replied, 'each morning, noon and night. This is how you do it. Repeat each scripture three times: three times in the morning, three times at noon and three times at night. That means each verse will be repeated nine times a day. I would like you to do this for a week, at least.'

'What do you mean, "repeat"? Do you want me to read them?'

'Yes, but not silently; read them aloud. And direct your reading. Read the verse the first time to yourself, as if you were saying, "Fred, this is for you." Then, read it addressing the Lord. "Lord, this is your Word. You said so." The third time read the verse to the devil. Use it like Jesus did. "It is written . . . This is not my word, but God's Word, devil." Read aloud these scriptures this way three times a day.'

Fred didn't say a word. He just carefully tucked the prescription in his Bible.

'Now, Fred,' Elmer continued, 'we are going to pray. First, we'll praise the Lord for the power he has given us over the enemy. Then, Dr Harkins and I are going to agree in prayer and take the authority God has given to every believer and bind the enemy. (Matt. 18: 18–20; Luke 10: 19) Then we will loosen you, so that you can use these scriptures and be healed. The

Lord is right here with us and he will not let the enemy hurt you any more.'

Elmer knew that if he informed Fred step by step of the procedure, he would be less tense and become involved in the ministry. He was endeavouring to excite an active faith in the frightened man.

The two men, one on either side of Fred, began to express a strong confidence in the Lord. They praised God for the authority that had been given by Jesus Christ the Lord. (Matt. 28: 18–19) They worshipped the enthroned Saviour. They praised the name of Jesus. (Phil. 2: 9–11)

Fred sat quietly praying. He was not enthused. Fear was still the tyrant. The other two men prayed on. Faith was rising. They thanked God for the authority in Jesus' words and works. They knew the authority that the Father had given Jesus over all the principalities and powers. He had defeated the enemy at the time of his death on the cross and that victory was attested by his resurrection. (John 14: 10–11; Col. 2: 15)

Fred stirred, uneasy in his chair. The mention of the cross and the power of Jesus' shed blood seemed to slightly disturb him.

The men prayed on, giving thanks to God for the indwelling power of the Holy Spirit. Not only did the Father give Jesus power in heaven, but through regeneration power was in them and in every believer. (John 16) Christ was sharing his victory over Satan. He would work through them to help Fred.

On the other hand they knew what they were up against. They faced a cunning, crafty deceiver. They were not only in the presence of the tormented man for whom they were praying, they were in the presence of the invisible powers of darkness. So they dealt in a very matter-of-fact way with the wily one.

Elmer declared, 'Lord, we know Satan is bruised under your feet. He is under our feet, too. We thank you that as the Father sent you, he has also sent us. You have said so, and we believe it.' There was no fear in the two believers. They were strong in the Lord and the power of his might. They knew they faced a defeated enemy. (Luke 10: 19; Rom. 16: 20; John 17: 18; Eph. 6: 10)

'I speak to the enemy who has deceived this man. You know that I know that you have no right here. He is God's child. He is redeemed by the blood of the lamb who died on the cross. I know you are defeated and therefore you are usurping a position here that is not rightfully yours. Fred has confessed his need of Jesus. We are confessing our faith in Jesus Christ to meet that need. You have no right here. Neither do you have a place here any more. Fred is going to read the Scriptures. Jesus cast your kind out with his Word and he will do it again. You know, devil, how you hate the Word, so you will not be comfortable here any more. You will have to stop oppressing this man when he reads the Word. He is the temple of the Holy Ghost. He is the Lord's. He belongs to Jesus. (1 Cor. 6: 13–17, 19–20)

'With the authority given by the Holy Ghost, and as a believer sealed with the Spirit of God, redeemed by the blood of Christ, I bind you and all your kind. You must not torment this man. I loosen Fred to read the Word of God. I free him to receive the help of the Holy Spirit. He is loosened to be as free as Jesus died to make him. In Jesus' name . . .' (John 15: 3)

Both men lovingly placed an arm around Fred. They encouraged Fred to have faith in Jesus' name. They claimed freedom from the binding and blinding that fear had caused. (1 Cor. 6: 19–20)

Elmer was emphatic. 'We know you seek a place to do your evil work in men and women. But you have no place in a sanctified Christian. You are a thief who breaks in, but we are forbidding you to remain or re-enter. You seek your own place, but don't touch a child cleansed by God. Go where you please under the limitations God has set and as Jesus allowed.' (Matt. 8: 28–34)

They bound all the depression that was united in an effort to imprison Fred in . despondency. (Matt. 16: 18–20; John 11: 44; Ps. 146: 7–8) Then they prayed for Fred to exercise his liberty by faith.

Fred began to weep and his weakness poured out in confession to God. Together the men claimed the mercy of God and his forgiveness. (John 20: 23) Together they claimed strength for Fred as he tried to carry through with the scriptures.

It was aggressive prayer, and they all knew that it had prevailed. (2 Cor. 3: 4–10)

Two weeks later the buzzer sounded in the study again.

'Yes?' Elmer said absent-mindedly.

'It's Fred ...' Rosemary quickly reminded him, 'He's the man you and Dr Harkins prayed with two weeks ago.'

'Oh, what does he want?'

'He wants an appointment with you.'

'He probably needs some more counselling and some scriptures.'

'Oh, no!' Rosemary sounded a bit excited. 'He wants an appointment for an interview. He wants to enrol in Christian Life College next term.'

'What?' Elmer was just about to say, 'No way. Suggest that he waits a year,' but he hesitated. 'Well, I guess I can at least see him about it.'

When Fred walked into the study, Elmer hardly recognised him. His eyes shone, a smile wreathed his face. His whole person stood and moved differently. He was a free man.

'What's happened to you?' Elmer exclaimed.

'I used the scriptures like you told me. The prescription worked, just like you said it would. I've used them every day for the last two weeks. Now I'd like to come to Christian Life College.'

Elmer stared at the new man sitting across from him. 'Why?'

'Well, you told me that I should have some other interests.'

Fred was challenging him with his own advice. After discussion and prayer Elmer said, 'Come. God needs you.'

If a spiritual health chart had been made for Fred, the line would have gone up and down, but always climbing during those next months. There were some behavioural symptoms of the past but the sickness was gone and Fred was healed. He was subject to depression and found it difficult to make up his mind. The habit of indecision was reinforced by his loneliness. He told Elmer about a girl-friend whom he had known for four years.

'We want to get married but I can't make up my mind.'

Elmer said, 'If you can't, no one else should. I'm not going to tell you whether to marry or not. That is something you two will have to work out.'

'She lives in the midlands. I go up to see her and when I'm there I am happy. It seems right that we should marry. When I come down here, where I'm alone again, I waver and get worried. I've changed my mind several times.'

'Indecision is a killer. It kills love and joy. You'd better make up your mind. Go up there and talk it over. The two of you pray together about it and then make a final decision together.'

The next week Fred came up to Elmer before class, beaming. 'We're engaged.'

8
How to live in the Overlap

Fred was learning to live in the Overlap. Like most of us, he didn't realise that his old life-style was not completely and immediately eliminated at new birth. He was learning a new life-style within God's kingdom through biblical revelation, but he was also remembering a lot of patterns he had learned in his past experiences. The unforgettable past and the present revelation create a new learning experience that can only be described as conflict. Fred was in the middle between the old and the new. The old life patterns and the new life goals produced a new learning experience within the Overlap.

Through learning experiences we mature in the Overlap. Spiritual growth is a result of getting to know God and his ways. In the old life our experiences were limited to our natural faculties. Now, in the new, we have spiritual vision and hearing. We develop new tastes and sensitivity. Awareness is heightened to comprehend spiritual realities. We begin to respond to our daily experiences in the light of what we have seen in the Bible; what we know by faith; what we sense in our spirit. We begin to discern by the power inside us.

Spiritual discernment is a wisdom revealed to those who live in the Overlap. The Holy Spirit is the revealer. He is given to us and he unveils, explores and examines so that we can comprehend and appreciate

Recognition

the significance of everything in the kingdom of God. The spirit of revelation opens our minds to recognise what is against us as well as what is for us within the Overlap.

Through challenging conflicts we learn that conflict, change and conquest are components within our new life. We discern that the world, the flesh and the devil are with us in the Overlap.

Within the Overlap we are on a battlefield and we are part of a present-day war. Through biblical revelation we discern our equipment and weapons to fight a good fight of faith. We must recognise that we are in a danger zone, but it need not be a disaster zone. We, the new creation, have been in the mind of God from the beginning. He sent his Son to bring us victoriously into the Overlap. He has brought us in free, through the power of his cross. Faith in Jesus is the way the victory of God is received. We must make unconditional surrender to the verdict of God pronounced on Jesus Christ. The verdict is that Jesus is victor. To surrender is to believe. The only way to enter into the victory of God is through the work of God accomplished by Jesus Christ upon the cross. We are justified by our faith in him. When we believe, God's righteousness is imputed, pronounced upon us, and our guilt is lifted.

Since we are all partakers of such amazing grace through the saving work of Christ, we have a special dignity to live holy lives for God. We sanctify ourselves, or choose to take the steps apart from our own self-centredness, to follow Jesus. Our sanctification is expressed in the mutual responsibility we share as brothers and sisters in the same family. We all recognise that we are sons, who were once slaves, and so we begin to be merciful to one another. In so doing, we step into the role that Jesus sanctified us to take.

We take his victory over Satan. We recognise Jesus as the stronger man, living in our flesh, who overcame our accuser here in our world. We share his glory at the throne, where we have been acquitted. By faith we seize the free grace, given once for all. We determine that our lives will reveal his victory. As overcomers we hear the shout of our King in the Overlap.

We see the enemy now as a defeated foe. He is the terrorist, who, with all his organisation, is under house-arrest, awaiting the final sentence that will imprison him for ever. We recognise that we have authority, as soldiers of the King, to restrain the enemy. We have an armour and weapons that enable us to exercise our God given authority.

The believer, justified and sanctified, sees himself as child of the King. Dominion has been given to his Saviour, and he steps into his victory. He undertakes to establish the kingdom that is already within him, in his world. He moves into the world to restrain corruption, overcoming evil with good. He tells them and he shows them the good news of the kingdom. He lives with duel citizenship and neither one exempts him from his responsibility to the other.

The believer recognises himself not only as a son, but as a priest for his Lord. He ministers as his servant, by the working of God's power within. He is equipped to be a minister, first of all to the Lord, then to others. His abilities are divinely bestowed. They are upbuilding and interdependent upon the abilities of others within the family of God.

As he minsters, he is vigilant and powerfully anointed to act as a soldier for his King. He overcomes the foe within and restrains the foe without. He recognises enemy territory and seeks to set others free who are caught in the snares of the world. He wears his armour and uses his weapons with skill that is developed by daring to speak the word of authority. He treasures the meaning of his Saviour's blood, studies the Word of God and breathes the name of Jesus in a constant prayerful vigilance. He serves eviction notice to the enemy anywhere he finds someone who wants to be free of the intruder. He binds the powers of darkness and loosens the captives.

All of this is done by faith. The believer's faith in the Saviour comes as he identifies himself with Jesus at the cross, and his throne. He has faith in the victor who sends him the Holy Spirit to indwell him. The Holy Spirit then tells him he can be what God says he is.

Within the Overlap the world is seen in several ways. The created world is still recognised, of course. The sound Christian is fully aware of his natural environment. He also continues to see the world of people and recognises himself as part of the human race. He becomes more sensitive to the hidden power of the world of things and the worldly systems that support it. With spiritual discernment he discovers an invisible world, with its own ruler and organised forces working through the worldly system and affecting the world of people and the natural environment. He has an ever-growing revelation of the overall world of good that extends beyond earth and time, which has a plan and purpose that provides a special destiny for the whole world, the earth, its systems, visible and invisible.

The man who accepts the biblical revelation sees God as creator of the visible earth and all that is in it. By reason of creation he declares, 'This is my father's world.'

He also sees the world of people so loved that God gave his Son to live among them and die for their sins. Because the Son came into our environment and into our humanity the believer loves the world of lost sinners.

A new value-system develops through the discernment the believer has within the Overlap. The materialism the world calls reality is recognised as perishable and unprofitable, if given in exchange for the real life. He realises that preference for the world is an expression of rebellion against God. He senses in the world of things a power that could put him in bondage.

The biblical revelation emphasises an invisible world. Those who study the Scriptures see another world of evil within our atmosphere, which is ruled by Satan and inhabited by spirit beings who are organised into companies actively engaged in conflict against the world of people. Behind man's rebellion and rejection of God is the hatred of Satan. He is the god of this world of invisible forces that blinds the mind of humanity. He is the adversary of everyone. He slanders and destroys. He was created by God as an angel of light, but through pride he fell into devilry of darkness, taking with him a host of others who lost their angelic status. He is an actual personality, neither divine nor human, but real. He is the ruler of the invisible world of evil.

The invisible perspective is the centre from which the visible evidence of evil emerges. The inexplicable hostility, the unreasonable rebellion, the irrational hate that lashes out in violence, man against man and man against God, has a central source. It is the lying mouth of the ancient destroyer, Satan. His re-enacted in every individual. Unregenerated man is a prisoner within the system of rebellion against

God. His ignorance of the fact is evidence of his spiritual blindness. Rebellion has developed an organised system that is called 'this world'. It is the present world order of human existence, without the knowledge of God, that reflects the pride that alienates man from God. It is into this world that he sends us who know life in the Overlap.

Those who live in the Overlap are not living ignorantly, for they have the Scriptures. They know the power of Satan is limited. He is under house-arrest, awaiting sentence and imprisonment. Not only he, but all his hosts who share his evil work. Christians know that although he is strong, a stronger one has not only come into the world, but into the believer. Those who live in the Overlap are authorised and empowered to overcome the enemy and to release prisoners who wish to be free. They have an armour of light that enables them to enter enemy territory and to pull down the strongholds of evil. Their weapons are indestructible. They are the blood of Jesus, the name of Jesus, the Word of God and the Holy Spirit. Through these they unite under their head, the conquering Christ, and restrict the enemy by their prayers and preaching of the cross.

The flesh, along with the world, is part of our life in the Overlap. We would be less than human without it. The term 'flesh' can mean one of several things in the Bible. For example, it can refer to a mass population or it can mean a physical body. The most prevalent New Testament meaning is the human nature with its natural appetites.

Believers have a new life through regeneration, but the same human nature. They are not half-human and half-divine. Nor do they have two natures. They are totally human, but through the spirit they can partake of the divine nature of Jesus. He is divine, they are human. Without God the human nature is carnal. With God it is spiritual. When we lived outside the Overlap our human nature had strong appetites that were self-centred. Inside the Overlap we still have a human nature with strong appetites. The difference is that there is an alternative control centre. It is the new life centre of the spirit.

We can choose to let the Lord Jesus control the appetites of our human nature through the spirit, or we can decide to remain carnal and live according to the old patterns of the flesh.

The Holy Spirit within will help the new man in Christ to partake of the divine nature of Jesus. The Tempter, on the other hand, waits to take advantage of the carnal mind. We can either grieve the Holy Spirit and fall prey to the enemy, or we can resist the devil and be full of the Spirit. To live according to the flesh in the Overlap is death to the fruit of the spirit. To live according to the spirit is life and peace.

When conflict comes between the willingness of the spirit and the weakness of the flesh, recognise that you are a human being with two choices. You are the one who can decide whether you will be carnal or spiritual. In your mind are the habits of the body and the soul, most of them developed when you knew nothing of the power of the spirit. By your choice to obey the spirit you are able to partake of the divine nature of Jesus and renew your mind. By the knowledge of the Word of God we learn what is the will of God. Obedience to the word and will of God develops a new life-style and we recognise that more and more we have the mind of Christ.

We are still in this world and in the presence of sin

and the devil. We can be influenced by all of them, but they do not have control of us. The devil can do no more than influence us. Like sin, he has no more dominion over us. We are free to choose whom we will serve.

9
The Inside Nudger

One winter day I boarded a train in Cardiff, Wales, after a busy weekend of ministry at Bethel Temple. I was on my way to Liverpool, so I looked for an empty compartment where I might rest undisturbed. Sliding the door open I slipped into the first cubicle. I like the English trains with their small compartments that hold six to eight passengers, seated across from one another. It can be a good opportunity to chat and share some good news about the Lord, except that day I just wanted to rest. I was nodding off, snug in my warm corner, when the train slowed and jolted to a stop.

'Oh Lord,' I prayed, 'if I'm to be alone, don't let anyone come in, but if you have someone that needs to hear of your love, then let them in.' Moments later a woman passed, looked in and walked down the narrow passage. No one else came by. I snuggled down into my corner, rested my head against the side of the car and closed my eyes. The door slid open with a growl and a bang, as if angry at the intrusion. The woman who had walked by had come back. She was small, around thirty-five, with a tiny face poking out from a woollen head-scarf. She avoided me, her eyes looking around me, above me, but never at me. She settled herself into the opposite seat and fixed her stare out of the window, but I felt that she was not seeing what was there. She was looking through it to what she had left behind, or was it what lay before her? I wondered. I closed my eyes to sleep, rather glad that my fellow passenger had so obviously hung out the 'Do not disturb' sign. Then the Holy Spirit nudged me. Deep inside he reminded me of my prayer. 'If you have someone that needs to hear of your love, let them in.' She sat very still hiding in the shaded waters of her thoughts. I tried to get her attention and dangled some bait.

'Nice scenery along here.'

She nodded, barely looking at me.

'Do you come from this part of the country?' I asked.

'Yes.' She didn't move nor turn from looking out of the window.

'I'm not from these parts ...' I would have continued, but she shot me such a quick frightened look that I stopped. Her dark eyes seemed to plead with me not to make her talk, just to leave her alone.

'Right,' I thought. I had no desire to be ill-mannered and thrust my company upon this poor, unwilling soul. She probably mistrusted Americans.

'You prayed that if someone needed to hear of God's love that he would send them in. Well, here she is ... go on Jean, tell her,' the Inside Nudger said.

'I bet you can't guess why I'm in this country.' I prodded her, flashing as big a smile as I could manage.

She glanced at me, obviously surprised that I had the audacity to try again. She was determined to discourage the conversation. 'No,' she said.

'Oh why don't you try. Go on,' I was unmerciful and smiled even more. She turned from the window and looked at me. With a weary voice she said, 'I suppose you are here on holiday.'

'No, not in February.' I chuckled, like I had said something funny. She didn't smile. We rode in silence for several seconds.

'Go on, try again.'

'Are you visiting friends?' Her voice was a little warmer. She was giving up, ready to tolerate me, like one would an ill-mannered child.

'Well, they are not my friends when I arrive, but usually they are when I leave.'

She looked seriously concerned, as if she worried about my sanity. I hoped she wouldn't leave the compartment. I hurriedly cast my line.

'Oh, I don't suppose you would ever guess, for I am a preacher and I'm speaking in churches all over Britain. Do you go to church?'

The bait worked. She snapped, 'No.'

'Oh that is too bad. What happened?'

To my surprise she leaned forward and began to talk in a confidential tone and I knew I had caught her for the Lord.

'I went to church up to recently. Then I began to have some trouble with my husband. He left me and I didn't know how I'd manage with two kids. I went to the vicar to see if he'd help me somehow. Well, he just looked at his watch several times and seemed so uninterested, like he couldn't care less. It made me mad. It wasn't easy for me to go in there and talk to him that way. I could see that I was taking his time from something else, so I got up and when I left I vowed I'd never darken the door of a church again. And I haven't.'

She paused, as if that was the end of the story, there was no more to tell. I was sure there was.

'Oh,' I said, 'you made the same mistake that a lot of us have. I did the same thing. I thought the church should have the answers and solve my problems. But you know the churches we go to are the sign-posts along the road. They just point the way to the one who can help us. Some churches do it better than others. But if you look to the Church alone you'll be disappointed. When you find a sign-post you haven't found your destination. You're just on the way.'

She listened attentively, as if she wanted to hear some reason for why things had gone as they had.

I continued. 'You know, I don't think it was an accident that you and I came into this car. I believe the Lord heard you asking for help and he sent you and me here to meet so I could tell you about his love.'

For miles we talked about Jesus. Our compartment was like a chapel. He was there and when we prayed he met her. With tears she thanked him for loving her and asked him to come into her heart. The inward change was transforming. Her face glowed with joy. Excitedly we talked of the prospects of her new life in Jesus.

'Why, you and your husband can get together again. God will give you a new love for him,' I told her.

Her face darkened. 'I don't ever want to see him again.' She was bitter.

'Well, don't worry about that for now,' I said quickly, before she slipped back into her dark thoughts. I knew the Holy Spirit would take care of that matter in her. We looked at the Scriptures and talked about her two little boys.

Finally she said, 'You know, I didn't tell you, but I got a letter from my husband a while back. He begged me to come home and for me to forgive him. He misses the boys. But I've been so hurt and he never wrote or anything for two years. I wrote back 'No ...' and then we decided we should get a divorce. That's why I'm going to Liverpool, to see him at the solicitor's.'

98

No wonder it had been so hard for her to talk about the scenery. She went on, 'Now, I think I'll talk to him alone before we go to the solicitor's office. Maybe it will make a difference if I tell him what has happened to me.'

We were praying about that when the train pulled into Liverpool station. Throughout the journey no one else came into the compartment, not even the conductor to punch my ticket. Good thing too, for I discovered that I had mistakenly gone into a first class car, rather than a second class.

It was months later when her letter caught up with me. She told me that she had phoned her husband as soon as she arrived in Liverpool She asked him if they could have dinner together that night. He was so slow in answering that she feared he would hang up. He agreed and later at the restaurant she told him of how she had found Christ on the train. He seemed preoccupied with the food on his plate, hardly looking at her. When he did look up there were tears in his eyes.

'You know when you phoned at the hotel? Well, I was sitting on the edge of the bed with a gun in my hand. There didn't seem to be any use in living without you or the kids. I'd made such a mess of everything. I was trying to get the nerve to blow my brains out when the phone rang. I couldn't believe my ears when I heard your voice.'

The letter closed, 'Thanks so much for being persistent with me on that train. I'm so glad you didn't give up. We're all serving the Lord now ...'

10
How to help others to live in the Overlap

We can get an 'I don't feel at home' attitude to our place in this world. It is true that we are pilgrims and strangers, but we are not just passing through. Our contact with the world should not be a necessary evil to be endured on our journey to a better land. Some Christians can get so intent on getting along in their Christian train of activities and fellowship, that they fail to linger with the world any longer than necessary to gather as many unbelievers as possible, who then have to move quickly to keep up with all our schedules and regulations.

There are the commuter Christians on a non-stop trip to glory. Think of what they miss. They forfeit the excitement of meeting people, many who have lost their way at different stations of life. How boring their Christian experience must be. They cannot share in the hustle and bustle, the jostling and shoving of the real life in the Overlap. Of course, it must seem safer to simply sit in their own quiet kind of fellowship where there is no flashing conflict, just a slow burning boredom.

There is a difference between the commuter Christian and the communicator Christian. The communicator is not so safe. His inner new life flashes out a message that gets all kinds of reactions, some dramatically pleasurable and others traumatically ter-

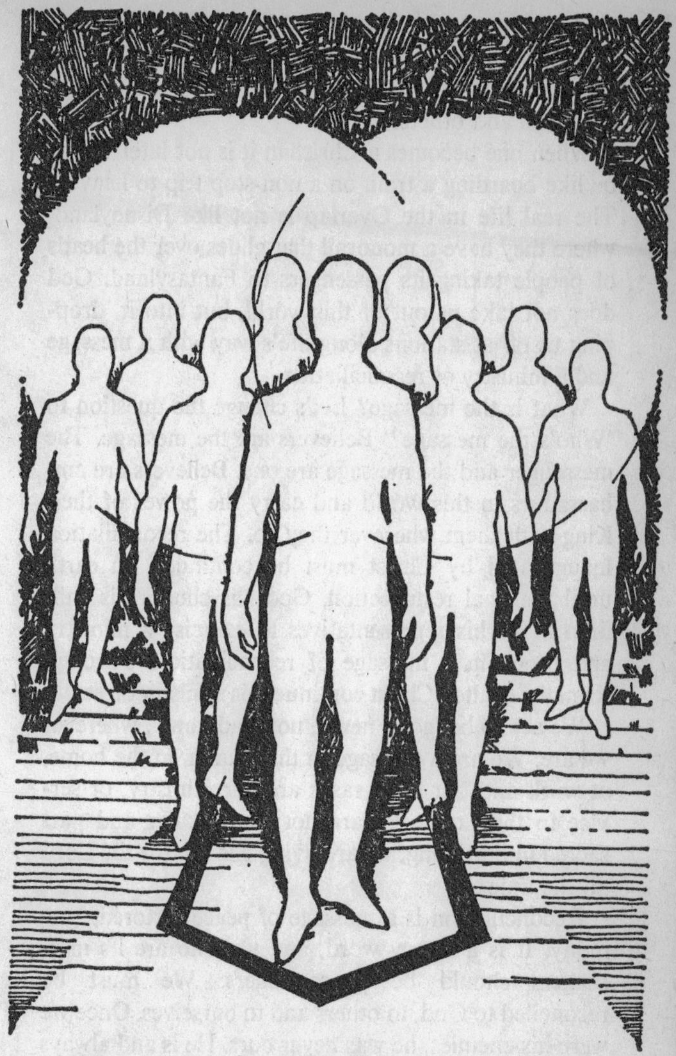

Reconciliation

rifying, but always exciting. Accepting or rejecting contact with the world around us, can be a life and death matter. We stand the risk of losing and saving ourselves and others.

When one becomes a Christian it is not intended to be like boarding a train on a non-stop trip to heaven. The real life in the Overlap is not like Disneyland, where they have a monorail that glides over the heads of people taking its passengers to Fantasyland. God does not take us out of this world, but into it, dropping us off at stations along life's way with a message and a ministry of reconciliation.

What is the message? Let's change the question to 'Who's the message?' Believers are the message. The messenger and the message are one. Believers are ambassadors in this world and carry the power of their King with them wherever they go. The reconciliation inaugurated·by Christ must be continued on earth until the final resurrection. God has chosen his children to be his representatives to exercise a ministry and proclaim a message of reconciliation. Through them the exalted Christ continues his ministry on earth.

We are to be 'good news', not 'bad news', wherever we are. We are a message in the church, in the home, at work and our daily tasks are our ministry, or service to the Lord. We are not part secular and part sacred in our living, we are living one life for the Lord all the time.

Reconciliation is a message of peace restored, harmony. It is a happy word, and we who are its messengers should be peace-makers. We must be reconciled to God, to others and to ourselves. Once we were his enemies, he was never ours. He is and always has been our friend and our Father. He brings us back. Before we can be good news, we must be persuaded to

102

fully return to God. Our peace is made at the cross through the atonement of Jesus. Atonement is a result of love. It was God's love for the world and people that determined Jesus' mission. Through the atonement on the cross God no longer counts our trespasses against us. Having justified us, he can trust us with being the message of reconciliation. Do we trust ourselves? Are we at peace with ourselves sufficiently to act as a message of peace and harmony?

Sin makes us ashamed of ourselves, and often after we have been regenerated and have moved into the Overlap we cannot shake off the feeling of being unworthy or unlikely to be used of God. Failure has made us mistrust ourselves. Some have loathed themselves. While they may not attempt self-destruction with a lethal weapon, they continuously whittle away the potential of their new selves with self-condemnation.

God has made us the kind of people that need no longer be ashamed of themselves. We need no longer fear to express ourselves, for there is no need to hide or cover up. We are not fearful because our sin is covered by the atonement, God has made us to live abundantly with plenty of love and peace. We can function effectively – physically, spiritually and mentally – in the power of the new life. This is not fantasy nor wishful thinking, nor even positive thinking. It is believing the truth of God's word.

Repentance is facing up to ourselves. If we have done that, then we know that we are what we are by the grace of God. We recognise ourselves, because we recognise our Saviour. Some are unable to function as 'good news' in this world because they are so preoccupied with self-inspection. 'Know thyself' philosophy is good up to a point, but you can know yourself too well. Anyone can become overwhelmed with inner uncleanliness, unreliability, inconsistencies and conflicts. When faced with these we should repent and turn ourselves over to God for cleansing. Then begin to see ourselves as we are in Christ. See our redeemed selves, our re-created selves. 'Know yourself and your Saviour' is the philosophy of the cross. Of course we have weaknesses, but he has strength. Yes, we have problems, but he has promises. Let us see ourselves and believe what God says about us. We are not what the past says we are, nor what our memory says we are, nor what the devil says we are. In fact, the devil doesn't have to say much to us. We talk to ourselves and say it for him. Instead, let's direct our desires, set our faith, fix our hearts on being a message of good news in this world. If we can doubt, then we can believe. If we can worry, then we can trust. We learnt to lie to ourselves so we can learn to speak the truth to ourselves. Let's turn our believing around. It is no more difficult to believe now than to remember the past or to worry about the future. Be reconciled to God. He loves us so let us love ourselves. If we do, it won't be so hard to love our neighbours.

Fear of self-acceptance results in non-acceptance of others. Life becomes humourless. We lack a reasonable faith and expectancy for anybody or anything to change. If we have a reversed faith for trouble and sickness, we need to tell somebody else in the Overlap, someone in the family of God. For our ministry and our message is not a solo performance. We are a family with unusual abilities and inheritance to share with one another.

Before we can be a message of peace to the world around us, we must be at peace within the family, whether it be our church family or the family that shares our house. That does not mean a neutral

104

pleasantness that camouflages our deep, personal feelings. We cannot fake our lives in the Overlap. If we do, we have nothing to say to the world outside. If your present family, at home or in the church, make you feel guilty because of your problems, then ask your heavenly Father to lead you to someone who will listen to you. If there is no one then let the Holy Spirit reveal to you that your faith will not fail. He believes that you will be changed so much that you will be able to strengthen others in the family.

When you pray, ask both God and the family to forgive you. Forgive those who are legalistic and hard. Forgive them for their oppressive demands upon you. Forgive yourself for not being just like Jesus. Face up to it, for it is unrealistic not to. Jesus is not reproducing little images of himself, like wind up toys. He is producing a family who bears his likeness but each member is as much himself as they were before he changed them. Ask God to forgive you for repressing your dark thoughts and feelings when you pray, or when you have a chance to share with a loving brother and sister in the family. Ask him to help you speak openly and to have friends with whom you can be yourself. You may have to look for them outside your church, I hope not. If you do, you will be likely to bring them, by God's love, into the Overlap, because of your honest real life before them. Real Christians are good news.

Our daily submission to the lamb on the cross gives us the authority of the lamb on the throne. The cross on the earth, within our human experience, gives us access to the throne in heaven, within the biblical revelation. This is the message and ministry of reconciliation within the Overlap.

Authoritative ministry is developed by directed

believing. We believe the truth as we see it in Jesus Christ. We identify with him at the cross and at the throne. Our believing is expressed by the word of faith in our mouth. We can speak it because we believe it. We turn our believing from the untruth to the truth. The truth declared by the ambassador of the cross is the word of his King. That word and the person of Jesus is so united and alike that they are inseparable. He is Truth.

We are not only authorised to act in this world in his name, but we are also empowered. Just as the word of authority is incarnate in the person of Jesus, so the power we have is not abstract, but a person who is personally ours. We are sent with the Spirit of God into the world. By our obedience to the Son we receive power to establish peace among people. We establish the kingdom of God, so that his will is done on earth as well as heaven. So the kingdom is not a matter of talk, even authoritative talk, but of power. We bind the enemy of men's souls by our words of faith in Jesus' name, and we loosen captives by our ministry of love. We minister love to one another in fellowship and support. We minister love to the world by our communication, our witness. We demonstrate the goodness of him whom we love. In the past we had no identity with God, now we do and so we pass the good news to others. We have received mercy, not at arms' length, but intimately, from God. Now we pass it on through the intimate ministry of reconciliation. That intimacy is the cross we bear in our ministry. It is hard on the flesh. To go to people, to speak to them, touch them, love them, give up yourselves for them, even to die for them, that is our ministry and message of reconciliation. There is where we weep and bleed and where we see the miracles of love.

11
Faith to hold on or to let go

I drove through Regents Park, round and round, to build up the battery. I cried a little. Everything seemed to take so much effort and I was so tired.

It was the day before I drove to Odell, Bedfordshire, for the Greenbelt Music Festival. Elmer was attending an Educator's Conference in Derby, our secretary was on vacation and I had a lot to do to get ready. In a big hurry, as usual, I had rushed down to the parked car. I was late for my appointment at the hairdresser. Besides, the traffic warden was coming, and since we didn't have a garage we had to keep feeding the meter every four hours, just like caring for a baby. The key didn't work too well in the car door, I struggled with it. It clicked; I jerked the door open and slammed it as I plopped behind the wheel and pushed hard on the accelerator. I turned the key. Nothing happened. I tried again, groaning, 'Oh no.' The creaking of the pedal and the click of the key was all I got for all my frantic pressure on the pedal and fervent prayer, 'Lord make it start.' No answer from the Lord nor the car. I leaned over, resting my head on the wheel. The tightness between my shoulders sent sharp pains up my neck. A persistent pressure pounded behind my right eye and pushed inside my ear. A dull thud throbbed in the back of my head.

Feeling that all the neighbours were watching from

behind their windows, I slowly got out and locked the car. Every step across the cobbled mews jarred my brain and beat like a drum in my head. Slowly I climbed the four floors to our flat. I'd have to cancel the hairdresser's appointment and call the AA to come and charge the battery. 'We've had nothing but trouble with that car,' I muttered. 'Where's that AA card?'

'Well, there it is; going all right now.' The AA man had only taken a few minutes, but I had had to wait an hour and half before he came. When I gave him my card to fill in his work slip he said, 'Oh your membership has expired. You'll have to pay four pounds.' 'Here goes my hair-do,' I thought. 'You'd better drive it round the park right away and charge the battery,' he advised me. So, here I was going round and round. As the tears rolled down my cheeks I thought how the dead battery and the circles I was going in illustrated my life. I was running on a weak battery, quickly charged by the discipline of day-to-day duties. Just making it was the way of life for me. But where was it leading? Would I start some day and find that there would be no power to tick over as usual? I felt that could happen at any time or any place.

What a year it had been. Elmer and I had finally pulled out of the difficulties following our transition from Post Green to London. It was a vast change, moving from the rural, close community life we had there in the green hills near Poole harbour to the spreadout city life among the grey, unfamiliar streets of London. Our greatest trial had been the uncertainty of where to live. It had deeply affected us. We were embarrassed by our muddled guidance; failing three times to find a place. Anxiety, tension and exhaustion resulted.

I had found it hard to minister in London. I missed the Post Green fellowship. We had no team here, as we did there. It took a while to develop new living and work patterns. But gradually friends began to draw close to us and if it had not been for a ladies' prayer group and the faculty and friends at the college, I don't know what we would have done. Then, God graciously gave us a flat through the generosity of a young business man. Through all of the hassle of moving I had constantly had difficulty in prayer. Every event, each time of ministry, even the ordinary day-to-day things demanded such determined effort. Enjoyment turned into duty. I was disciplined to persevere, no matter how I felt. Without that discipline I couldn't have made it.

That is how I got through my tour in Australia. I'd had forewarning from doctors in Dorset that I needed surgery to stop haemorrhaging due to fibroids. When I was in Melbourne I haemorrhaged so badly that I thought I would have to return to England. However, with my Australian friends' help I was able to carry on, even going on to the highlands of New Guinea.

As soon as I returned we began the month's IF MY PEOPLE tour of Britain from Truro to Glasgow. By the time our group of fifty had reached the Royal Albert Hall in London we'd travelled 2,113 miles, ministered to over 22,000 people in 13 performances in 15 days. We still had the other half of the tour to go, which included Belfast and Dublin.

Our ministry in London had priority, so along with these major events, including teaching sessions for Youth With A Mission in Europe, Elmer and I carried on in the city to which God had called us. We both lectured at Christian Life College. I sat on different committees; The Nationwide Festival of Light Executive and a sub-committee organising a specialised ministry to homosexuals addicted to pornography. Also, there were the London area ministers' meetings, The Fountain Trust Advisory, plus a series of weekly services in Wandsworth and Notting Hill Gate.

As I drove round and round Regent's Park trying to charge the battery, I wondered what I could do to get myself recharged. I felt so tired. I'd been battling with headaches, backaches, muscular tension in my neck and shoulders so long that I had grown accustomed to not feeling well. That is, until I'd start haemorrhaging and then the struggle was intensified and unbearable. When that would start terrible black thoughts shadowed my mind. Everything became negative. I found it hard to think, or to make decisions. Often I'd get so nauseated I'd vomit green bile. My weakness made me melancholy. I became nervous and could hardly bear anyone to be near me. Crowds were all right, as I could stand apart and minister. During those times I could switch over to the message and ministry of the Holy Spirit and my personal problems and weakness were forgotten. But I couldn't bear being alone with anyone, I felt threatened, actually afraid.

'Well,' I thought, 'I hope Greenbelt will do me good, and I'll do it some good. The crowd should be big enough for me there.' They were expecting twenty-five hundred. I had been working on the planning committee for the musical festival all year and was to do some teaching there.

'I'd better get going. The battery should be O.K., and I hope I am.' I turned and drove out of the park.

Strange how one will drive faster when upset. I wanted to get to Greenbelt as soon as I could. I was feeling worse by the mile and I wondered if I was going to make it. As I left the motorway to follow the ever-narrowing roads towards Odell, my head began to throb. Suddenly, like someone switching a light off and on, I couldn't see for a split second. Then abruptly everything was back again. A momentary blank; it terrified me. I slowed down, blinking my eyes and praying that I would make it to the Greenbelt Festival. If I could just get there and rest, then I'd be fit to speak for the sessions we'd planned. I was weak and dizzy and then it happened again; the total darkness came and went.

I was pulling the car towards the side of the road when I saw two people just ahead. One fellow had a guitar slung over his shoulder and the girl was carrying a sleeping bag. Both were loaded down with camping gear. I was sure they were on their way to Greenbelt. As I passed them they waved. I backed the car. They started to run towards me, their faces full of smiles. 'Would you happen to be going to Greenbelt?' I asked.

'Yes, we sure are.'

'Hop in and I'll give you a lift.' As they unloaded and started to stash the stuff in the car, I asked the boy, 'Would you like to drive?'

'Me? Oh yes.' He was delighted.

We pulled into the tree-lined lane leading across the open fields to the camp site. Peter, the director, met me. 'Peter I'm not well, and I must go straight to where you've put us up.'

'Right. It's just across the road, only a few yards down from the entrance of the lane. It's called Rill Cottage.'

I cautiously pulled into the cottage driveway, leaned back and sighed. I'd made it. 'Thank you Lord, thank you for getting me here. Just get me to where I can lie down and rest.'

The oak door of the white English cottage opened. Elmer came out. He had arrived before me, coming directly from the conference in Derby. As he opened the car door he said, 'Good, you're here. Wait till you see this place. You'll love it. Mr and Mrs Campbell have done a terrific job renovating three small cottages and combining them to make a ranch-style house. The walls are really thick, painted white with dark oak beams. Just what you like. The fireplace is cone-shaped and made of stone. And . . .'

'Elmer', I broke in. 'I'm really tired. I don't feel good at all.' He took a good look at me, lifted the suitcase and said, 'Let's get inside. There's a cup of tea waiting.'

Mrs Campbell was understanding when I asked if I could go to our room rather then lingering over the home-made scones and tea.

'You rest my dear, and we'll have a salad plate before you go over for the opening of the festival.'

We walked the short distance to the camp site. The night was wet and cold. The lane was full of cars lined up to the main road waiting to be registered for the festival. A thousand or more young people were sitting in the field wrapped in rugs and blankets or rolled up in sleeping bags. Elmer and I threaded our way through the humped forms to a spot in the middle. We sat on the ground and tried to get ourselves comfortable. I felt cold to the bone.

The stage seemed to be completely disorganised. Several people were still working on the lights, climbing ladders adjusting spots. Weird sounds erupted from the microphones as they were tested and moved around. It irritated me that this was done so late, with all those people sitting waiting in the cold. Then a voice boomed out above all the other stage noises and

112

announced the first group. Greenbelt Festival, for which we had prayed and planned all year, had started.

I got colder and couldn't stop shivering. My back hurt and although I leaned against Elmer for warmth and support, it became unbearable. Elmer said, 'I think we had better go back to Rill Cottage.'

It was a long night, with hardly any rest. I was haemorrhaging and in pain. At six-thirty as I weakly walked in from the bathroom, I clutched the door frame. A wave of unconsciousness billowed over me and my voice sounded far away as I called for Elmer. I couldn't stand or hold on any longer. My head hit the bedroom door as I fell to the floor. When I came to I was retching violently. Elmer was at my side.

'It's all right, honey. Just lie still.'

'The Campbells? What do they think of me? I'm causing so much trouble.' I tried to get up but I was too weak. Mr Campbell took one look at me and said, 'I'll go and make a cup of tea.' Elmer grinned. 'Typical British reaction.' Then looking more serious, 'Mrs Campbell has called the doctor.'

After an examination, the doctor called an ambulance and said I had to go to Bedford Hospital.

'What about Greenbelt?' I kept asking, but as no one answered I wasn't sure if I was speaking. My mind was so muddled that I felt out of reach. I was not able to do anything but let them carry me out of Rill Cottage and drive me away from the whole scene that I had struggled so hard to reach.

My eyes wouldn't open, but I could hear voices, feel hands working all around me, and kept wondering why I was allowing all this. I didn't want to be in this place. What had happened to put me in these people's hands? I was lying perfectly still, too weak to move, but my mind was rushing, planning how I could get out and back to Greenbelt. I'd never missed any speaking engagements, and I wouldn't miss this one. This sickness wouldn't last long. The Lord would touch me, as he had done before, and I would be back doing what I loved to do the most.

Then there was a blank when all was silent. I didn't feel or hear anything around me. A nurse's touch on my head woke me.

'You've had a blood transfusion. You'll start to feel better soon.' She and I smiled at each other and I was asleep. Later I woke for a few minutes and then was out again. Once again a voice awakened me.

'You've had another transfusion. You'll be feeling a lot better now.'

Weariness wrapped me up for another long sleep.

Later the doctor came straight to the point. 'You have fibroids. One is very large. You'll have to have a hysterectomy as soon as possible.'

Elmer made the plans for me to return to London. I was feeling great. The transfusions had done a good job of restoring my strength. I felt better than I had for months. So I prevailed on Elmer to let me stop at Greenbelt and take one of my sessions before going on to London. He was uncertain and hesitated.

'I know it will be all right, honey. I'm sure that the Lord will help me. He gave me a message before I came and I feel I must deliver it.'

'O.K., but then we go straight to London. When we get there I'll call Dr Harkins. He'll know what to do next.'

'Next? Don't worry about that. I'm going to be all right.'

The sun was shining. Greenbelt was a tent town, colourful, active with people adjusting to their temporary nomadic life. The big meeting tent was full, over two thousand sitting anywhere they could squeeze in. They knew I had come from the hospital and what a welcome they gave me. Then we feasted together from God's spiritual store. They were so hungry, so eager to hear God's word; so ready to be led towards the Lord's will. We talked about the Christian attitude towards culture. My heart overflowed with love for them ... God's lambs. Hands reached up when I asked those who had burdens of sin to signify their need of prayer. Then all over the tent groups gathered and reached out to one another in loving prayer for God's forgiveness. When I left the tent I was tired, but satisfied that I had done the right thing.

Elmer and I returned to London. It was good to lean back and let him do the driving.

By the time Dr Harkins came to see me I realised that the transfusions were a temporary boost just to get me home. I was too weak to get out of bed. Depression had settled on me like a black fog. Elmer and Rosemary, our secretary, had taken over my diary. They were cancelling appointments ruthlessly. Every one they cancelled made me more depressed. It was like Samson getting his hair cut. I felt my strength leaving me. Was I giving in to circumstances or giving up to God? Why wasn't I fighting back? I felt too tired to even express my objections to anything.

Dr Harkins, a gently, soft-spoken man with a loving Christian spirit, ministered to me as he talked about my physical problems. 'I was thinking about the woman in the Bible who touched the hem of his garment, Jean. Have you thought much about her?'

'She is practically my patron saint,' I replied. 'I've

prayed many times for the Lord to heal me, just as he healed her. His power from day to day has kept me alive. I haven't just touched the hem of his garment but I've clutched it. I've been holding on for the last three years. I knew I had these fibroids, but I thought I'd beat nature with the change of life. But the things grew. God helped me to overcome the problems all along the way. He gave me strength to do what had to be done.'

'Perhaps the Lord doesn't want you to drag on like this anymore,' Dr Harkins suggested. 'Maybe it is time to do something about this yourself.'

Should I give up having held on for so long? There were so many who still needed help. My heart longed to reach the people who had never yet heard how God loved them. And there were so many discouraged Christians who needed help. Was it right for me to stop?

'The word "relinquishment" comes to me while I'm lying here. That means to give up, yield or to let go, doesn't it?' I queried.

'Yes, but not in a passive manner, it requires an active faith that says – you take over, Lord.'

'It's awfully hard to release my grip on everything I'm doing. But now maybe God wants me to relinquish and take time to get well. I've no strength left to struggle against this suffering. I don't know if I can accept this without feeling defeated and resenting God's will? Also, what will all the people think who know how I've believed and prayed for so many to be healed?' I was close to tears.

'I think they may realise that you are human, just as they are. I'm sure they will pray for you.'

'I feel wrong talking about my problems. It disgusts me that I even want to. My usual inclination is to

116

speak of the Lord's goodness, rather than my weakness.'

'I'm sure you are not taking pleasure in your sickness, but you are not denying it, either. Why don't you just offer yourself as you are to the Lord, for his will to be done.'

'But I don't understand ...' and I stopped, for I knew that trusting God is not necessarily understanding God.

Dr Harkins smiled. He seemed to sense that I was taking my hands off the situation.

'Jean, I've waited to see how you were feeling about this to make any final plans, but I have contacted one of England's best gynaecologists. He has agreed to see you as soon as possible. It is remarkable he is in the country, for he is usually lecturing abroad at this time of year. But you must promise me that you will not retreat if he says an operation is necessary. You must not change your mind!' Dr Harkins smiled, for he knew I was likely to back out if I felt the least bit better.

Everything was happening to manoeuvre me into relinquishing all. We prayed and I agreed. There would be no backing out.

Two days later, on a bright, sunny Friday, I saw the gynaecologist. I wasn't asked, I was told to come in on Sunday for an operation on Wednesday.

'Sunday!' I was ready to object, but before I could say another word the doctor was out of sight and a nurse was assigning me to a ward in the Soho Hospital For Women.

'Well, when I turn everything over to the Lord' I thought, 'this is the way it goes. I have nothing to say about anything. Oh well, I won't waste the time. I'll use the next few weeks to write my book.'

Relinquishment didn't come easy for me. I knew better how to resist.

Elmer helped me up the steps of the old grey hospital. I walked like an old woman. Not only was I weak, I was unwilling. Fear mixed with anger made me feel apprehensive and resentful. We paused before we went in.

'You're not going to an execution,' Elmer remonstrated. 'Think of it as a vacation.'

I smiled wryly.

We were directed to take the lift to the second floor. The lift turned out to be a quaint, Victorian cage-like elevator that plunged me into anxiety. I felt trapped and I was going down, rather than up. The gates opened and we walked into Princess Christian Ward.

A small nurse with a sweet oval madonna face said, 'Mrs Darnall?' I nodded. 'Your bed is there.' She pointed to one in the middle of the ward. A yellow curtain was drawn around the bed and I changed into a yellow cotton hospital gown. 'The colour is really appropriate Jean,' I thought. 'Why aren't you fighting? Where's your faith?'

The nurses kept me busy for the next few hours with questions, orientation around the ward, and finally dinner with patients who could sit at the table. I really didn't want to meet anyone, but then I thought, 'No one will know me here.' I was still feeling ashamed about having to come to hospital and was concerned about what Christians would think.

There were introductions and when I opened my mouth my speech betrayed me; they knew I was American. Questions followed: Do you live here? What are you doing in England? How did you end up here?

'I collapsed at a music festival.' I kept my answer vague.

'At Odell in Bedfordshire?' a woman named Ivy asked.

I nearly dropped my fork. My face felt hot, my throat tightened and I felt foolishly guilty. 'Yes,' I said reluctantly.

'I know,' she smiled, 'I live near there . . .' and a look of Christian recognition passed between us. I managed a weak smile. Suddenly I didn't want any dessert. Excusing myself I got back behind my yellow curtain. Pulling the covers around my ears, I muttered, 'Lord, now everyone will know that the lady who prays for the sick is in the hospital.' The Lord didn't say a thing.

Flowers and visitors began to flow in the next day. When Elmer came to see me he told me the latest news. He'd heard that the very day I got sick, Faith Lees, our dear friend at Post Green, had been rushed to the hospital with cancer of the kidney. I could hardly believe it. Faith was so active and healthy. When Elmer and I had lived at Post Green we often remarked about her vitality. 'Oh, I wish I was able to go to her. If only we could pray together.'

'There are others who are right there and they are praying. She is in good hands, so don't worry,' Elmer assured me.

'But I've been told that Don Double and Dennis Clarke are also seriously ill. Look, Don's an evangelist and has such a terrific ministry and Dennis has people praying all over the country through his Intercessors For Britain organisation. It's the devil, that's what it is. We're being struck down like flies.' I was agitated.

Elmer was calm. 'Don't blame the devil for everything. It looks to me as if all you folks who've been rushing around, working so hard, are a bit run down. I think the Lord may be in this more than the devil.'

There was nothing more for me to say. I knew somehow that he was probably right. He usually is!

Just before I went into the operating room the nurse came in with an extension phone. 'A long distance call for you.'

A dear familiar voice said, 'Hi, Mom.'

It was John calling from Van Nuys, California. Suddenly he was there in that ward. So was Ruby, his wife, and Sharolyn, our six-year-old grand-daughter. Then, another dear voice joined in; La Donna. I wept with joy.

'Oh La Donna, I've missed you so much since you went to the States.'

'If I had known that you were so sick, Mom, I would have come home.' She sounded worried.

'Oh no, we know you are in God's will there in the Life Bible College, so don't you worry. And John I know that everything is going to work out for all of you.' I tried to sound cheerful. It was hard to know what to say just before one goes into an operating theatre. I had never had the experience before. I knew I would be all right, but did they feel right about me having the operation? It seemed that John knew what was on my mind.

'Mom, now you must not be worried about anything. We know how you trust the Lord, and you just trust him now. This operation is the best thing that could happen. It will make you rest. You'll soon be back feeling better than ever.'

All the usual things well people say to sick people, but it meant so much to me right then. In another moment it was all over. They were gone. I was alone with the Lord. The yellow curtain was drawn around me. I picked up my Bible to read. 'O Lord, thou hast searched me and known me! Thou knowest when I sit

120

down and when I rise up; thou discernest my thoughts from afar. Thou searchest out my path and my lying down, and art acquainted with all my ways. Even before a word is on mý tongue, Lo, O Lord, thou knowest it altogether. Thou dost beset me behind and before, and layest thy hand upon me ... Whither shall I go from thy Spirit? Or whither shall I flee from thy presence?' (Ps. 139)

I lay there with my eyes closed. I knew he would go with me. Then I picked up the Bible and looked at the last sentence. 'When I awake, I am still with thee.' In quietness I lay feeling passive, assured. I sensed this must be the peace of God.

'Hello, Jean,' a voice gently spoke. My eyes opened with surprise. I didn't expect a visitor so soon before my operation. It was the vicar of St Mark's, Kennington, Nicholas Rivett-Carnac. We had come to know him well through our college at St Mark's.

'You looked so peaceful, I thought you might be asleep,' he said.

'I was resting in the Lord, Nicholas.' I smiled.

'When you spoke at the Fountain Trust recently, Jean, there was something you said that I've not forgotten. This morning I felt I should come and share it with you.' Nicholas opened his Bible.

'Like bread on the waters,' I remarked.

'Yes. Here is the scripture you used for your text: "Look to him, and be radiant; so your faces shall never be ashamed." (Ps. 34: 5)

Was the Holy Spirit speaking to me through this dear friend? Guilt had been heavy upon me. True or false, it was real. I felt so guilty for not overcoming this sickness. When circumstances forced me to cancel everything and submit to the operation, I felt guilty for being relieved. Even the peace I was enjoying a few moments before seemed illicit. Why did I feel so guilty?

Nicholas continued. 'You told us to take our masks off, and to look to the Lord. He knows what is behind the mask.'

The mask! What is my mask? I knew, as if it had been written on the wall, I knew it was pride.

'You told us to look to Jesus and not to look at our troubles.' Nicholas closed the Bible and stepped a little closer. 'You said, "If we look at trouble, we will have troubled faces. Look to the Lord, and be radiant."'

Nicholas prayed and left. I prayed on.

'Lord, all I really have to be ashamed of is my pride. I haven't meant to hide my true self from you or others. I don't want to have this mass of pretence, any more than I want this fibroid mass. Take it out of me, Lord. I have been afraid that the truth about my physical condition would hurt my testimony and hinder the gospel. I should know better, but that is the way it is. I recognise that I am an imperfect vessel of clay. Let me be genuine and real to everyone. I don't want to wear a mask. I don't want to hide anything – even behind my faith. I'd like to live without a mask, but help me Lord, for I am proud and stubborn.'

The prayer was not put together very well and was punctuated with tears. There were gaps of silence when I waited to hear my own heart speak, as well as my lips. Then, my mind warned me, 'Be careful, don't get too emotional, for you are unsettled now. You are probably just nervous and upset because of the pending operation. Better get a hold on your emotions.'

I talked back to myself. 'Yes, I am upset and probably it is because I am going to have this operation.

122

There is no doubt that it is affecting me. But that is not the only reason. God is talking to me. He's telling me things I have been too busy to hear. So I'm glad I'm here waiting for this surgery. I thank you Lord Jesus for this illness.'

The yellow curtain was jerked back. My nurse said, 'All right now, Mrs Darnall, are you ready for your injection?'

'Yes, I'm ready.'

She jabbed in the needle. 'This will put you to sleep. You'll not know anything until it's all over.'

'Thanks,' I said.

'Well, no one's ever thanked me for a needle before!'

I closed my eyes. She didn't know how thankful I was.

'Very straightforward, Mrs Darnall. It was a good operation.' The voice came from somewhere above me. I tried to answer but my words drifted away before I spoke them. I swam after them and slept on.

Drips and drains and all the usual sleeping and suffering followed. Flowers and visitors filed in to celebrate that it was all over. I was able to genuinely rejoice with them, for I accepted the real will of God, rather than what I had demanded.

Finally I was able to walk, not very well, but even though I looked like a woman in the Bible who could in no wise lift herself, I walked. As I came down the passage towards my ward, something went wrong. My chest began to hurt. I felt myself falling. Holding on to the wall, I called for the nurse inside the ward. Cold sweat rolled down my face. My hands were wet. Pain cut through my chest, down my right side, over my shoulder and around my neck. I was slipping to the floor, my whole body was in a vice-like grip of pain. It held me most of the night. In the morning cardiagram tests showed evidence of a heart attack and a blood clot in the right lung. The nurses had worked hard with me all night. Now they stood around my bed, smiling and looking worried at the same time. The doctors looked at the cardiagram. They all seemed to be waiting for something. Then another doctor came in and spoke to the sister of the ward. She then announced to me, 'We're going to take you over to the Middlesex Hospital. They are better equipped to help you there. So, we'll have to get your things together. Don't worry, we'll take care of it all.'

Before I could ask anything they were bundling me on to a stretcher.

'But ...'

'Never mind. It is the best for you, Mrs Darnall.'

'But, my husband ...'

'Oh, we have phoned him ...'

There he was. Elmer had been awakened at seven o'clock with a call to come to the hospital at once. He was grey with strain. He was trying to cheer me up and find out what had happened at the same time.

'It'll be all right, honey.'

I wondered as they hustled me out if I looked radiant. I felt physically pale, but there was no mask. I was not afraid.

At the Middlesex there were doctors, more nurses, more flowers, but no visitors for the next few days. Tests, X-rays and consultations along with attempt after attempt to find a blood vessel for an injection. After twelve unsuccessful attempts in one day, they gave up. They tried again the next day. Finally, success. Pain exhausted me, but when I slept I had vivid dreams that I couldn't forget. I dreamed that I was

124

driving when I ran out of petrol and stalled by the road. I tried to get Elmer, but couldn't reach him. I awoke, distressed. Then, the Holy Spirit said, 'He maketh me to lie down . . .'

Then I dreamed that I was riding a long, long escalator, like the ones in the London underground stations. I descended into darkness, it was so deep and long. When I reached the bottom, I thought, 'Where am I? What will I do?' Then, there was another escalator back up. I stepped on and gradually came back to the light. When Elmer came to visit me I told him, 'Don't worry. I know now that I'll be all right. No matter what happens, I'll come out of it.'

One of my doctors stopped as he hurried through the ward. 'Mrs Darnall, we feel you ought to go to a rest home to convalesce for a couple of weeks.'

'I don't think my husband would like that. I'd rather go home. He's had to do everything for himself. I need to get back on the job.'

'That is just what I'm meaning,' the doctor frowned. 'You have been through a lot, and we don't want you to undo the good that has been done. Your recovery is wonderful, but your heart has taken a lot. You need a good rest.'

'Rest? Why I've been in bed for weeks.'

His expression told me that once again I was not really going to have a choice. I could just imagine the rest home . . . a cold, Victorian mansion, with gales of wind blowing down the passages. Old men and women tottering around. Brisk nurses telling you what you could do and what you could not do. Regulations for everything. And the autumn rains had started, so what gardens there were would be no good. I felt I had been sentenced to Colditz.

The Middlesex Convalescent Hospital in Clacton-on-Sea was a huge red-brick Victorian building. It had a garden set in expansive grounds. It was not cold and although there were older men and women, there were also lots like me, not so old. I had been very depressed by some of the severe cases of senility around me at the Middlesex. I missed my nurses and doctors – even those from Soho had come to visit me when I was at the Middlesex. There were patients, too, to whom I had grown attached. There was Sylvia who owned a pub. She suffered from an incision that wouldn't heal. It abscessed and she had to have another operation. Yet she was so cheerful and wrote to me when I was moved to the Middlesex. 'Remember. Rome wasn't built in a day ... be patient.' There was Mrs Morgan whose bed was across from mine. She had no home to go to, so she just stayed on in the hospital, even though she was well. Another patient, Pat, had been in the hospital a year. She was incurable. She went around to the other beds and cheered up the patients.

It wasn't long until I knew and admired the friends at Clacton-on-Sea. At the dining table there was a Jewess, Jean, and an attractive Irish fashion model, Carmen. Then, there was Tom, a shy, sensitive, young man, and Lorenzo, who couldn't speak much English, and longed to return to his native Italy.

I had bouts of migraine and minor aches and pains, but I progressed steadily at Clacton. It didn't rain all the time, either, so I was able to enjoy a walk to the sea front. It was soon time to leave. My excitement mounted as the day drew closer. Finally, the morning came and I was having my final breakfast there at the big diningroom table with my friends. I reached out for the pepper and was seized with a sharp pain across my chest. I jerked my arm back.

126

'Are you all right, Jean?' Carmen asked.

'Oh, yes.' I sat very still. Was I all right? Sure, it was only a minor pain. It was gone already.

I reached out again. The pain shot through my left shoulder, across my chest. I waited. It stopped. Then, when I lifted my fork to take a bite of food, it grasped me all the way around my chest. I doubled over and felt as if I was strangling.

'Get her back up to her room.' One of the ladies at the table had called the matron, even though I protested. 'I'll be all right,' I insisted. I wanted to go home so badly.

'I'm falling, I'm falling.' My body jerked with convulsions. Foam worked out of the corners of my mouth. I couldn't get my breath. The sister held me up in her arms.

'Lord,' I gasped. 'Save Britain. Please, Lord, help these people. Lord, bless Britain.' I wanted my last breath to be a prayer for this land. It was two hours before I was quiet. Like a summer storm, the fury had struck suddenly and left abruptly. I lay back on the pillows, exhausted. Elmer came to take me home, but had gone without me.

They moved me into a little room where a lady had died the day before. I didn't even have a voice left to object. My vision was blurred. All that was distinct was the pain in my left arm. My hand was numb.

The door to the little room opened cautiously while the nurse was taking my temperature. A head peeked in, 'May I come in?' I didn't know the face. The nurse said, 'She is not to have visitors, sorry.'

He came on in. 'I'm Dr Davis, a friend of her own doctor, Dr Harkins. Sister said I could have five minutes.'

He was a slight man, around thirty-five. His quick

actions and cheerful disposition reminded me of a bird. 'You don't know me, but I know you. I was at Greenbelt. I heard you speak there. It was a great service.'

God had sent me a brother in the Lord, just when I needed him.

Jean, the Jewess, was the first one to come in after Dr Davis. She stood at the door, not even coming near me. 'I'm sneaking in,' she said softly. 'I just want you to know that when you got sick we prayed for you. I told the ladies at the table, 'If it was one of us, you know what Jean would do for us, don't you? Well, let's go into the TV Room and do the same for her. So, we prayed, each one in their own way.'

I couldn't speak. Jean had been pretty adamant about her religious philosophy. She was a liberal Jew, but not a regular at the synagogue. As I looked at her strong face, dark eyes, and mass of coal black hair, my heart filled with love for her. She had been a stranger days ago. I had felt afraid of her and wondered how I could talk to her about anything. Yet, she was the one who had organised a prayer meeting for me. I blinked back the tears.

'I must go. Don't you cry now, or the nurse will give me the dickens.'

Carmen was next. 'They told me you were looking a little better.' She closed the door carefully. 'I shouldn't be in here. You see, I am going to leave now, and I just had to see you. I'll be going on to Italy to do modelling there for a fashion house. Jean, you know when we went to church last Sunday?' (Carmen and a couple of others had gone with me to the local church. She was Catholic and it was her first time in a Protestant church.) 'Well, I thought it was interesting, but I really didn't get much out of it. Like you said, it was a

128

lot of information and not much salvation.' I remembered how disappointed I had been, for the preacher had talked only on the history of the denomination, rather than about Jesus. There were three people with me all really wanting the Lord, and he never spoke to their need, nor to them personally. 'I just want you to know that you have been telling me more about Jesus than that preacher. Oh, don't talk, Jean. I promised that I'd not make you talk. I just want you to know that I read your book *Heaven Here I come* and I've asked the Lord to come into my heart. I hope you'll pray for me while I'm away. I've never found the church, even my church, very relevant. But you've made Jesus real to me.'

I reached out for her hand. I whispered, 'I must pray now . . . with you.' She knelt down beside the bed. Her golden hair glowed in the light of the bedside lamp. God was so near.

She had hardly gone when Tom came tip-toeing in. He reminded me of a pixie. He had a gentle, child-like quality about him. He had been very sick, but was getting better. 'Now you must not talk to me, I'll talk to you,' he said. 'When you were waiting for the lift the other day, I overheard something that you said to Carmen. Apparently she said she didn't go to church because there were good people there and she felt that she was too bad to go. It's what you said that caught my attention. You said, "Oh you don't understand. The church is not a college for saints, it is a school for sinners. I don't go to church because I think I'm perfect or good, I go because I know I'm imperfect, there is nothing good in myself that would save my soul." Jean, that's what I feel. I am really no good. Yet, I feel that there is something worth saving. I'm a sinner. I just want you to know that those words helped me . . .'

Tom paused. He wanted to say more. I sensed he was reluctant to go on. He didn't want to upset me.

'Tom, Jesus loves us. He died for sinners like you and me. Let's pray.' When we finished, he turned towards me as he left . . . 'You know, if you hadn't got sick yesterday, I wouldn't have had a chance to see you like this. You'd be gone now. I'm sorry you had it so rough, but I'm glad we had a chance to talk.'

I rode, flat out, in an ambulance back to the Middlesex Hospital in London. It was a rough ride on a lumpy canvas stretcher resting on a hard bench. As soon as I saw my former doctors I asked, 'When can I go home so I can start to live?'

'Just a few more tests, Mrs Darnall.'

I prayed, 'Lord I'm willing if that is what you want, but if it isn't, please let me go home.'

About five-thirty, my doctor came in smiling, 'You can go home, if you like.' I swung my legs over the edge of the bed. She added, 'But you'll be in our Out Patient Clinic for some time.'

Home was a battlefield where I had to resist attacks of the old depression, the sense of inadequacy, the dread of being left out of things, yet frustrated when I had to be responsible to anyone. I felt terribly obstinate, unloving and unfeeling at times. It was difficult to communicate, for I felt no one could understand how I felt. Elmer was depressed by my actions. It had been a long, hard ordeal for him. We were both tired. I didn't feel I could help him. My heart seemed hard. Premonitions of invisible trouble filled me with dread.

For a month everything was difficult. I wore weariness like a robe. I couldn't get out of it. Then, I realised I was comparing myself to the way I was when I was well and able to do everything. I had to put the past in God's hands. I tried to leave it there. I stopped wasting time speculating as to whether I had done the right thing. In many ways I doubted my actions. I daily committed those doubts to him. I also let go of the future, the way I wanted to be, and accepted myself as I was that moment. It was relinquishment of the past and future. I began to live in the now. I was winning the battle on the home front.

12
The unfinished life in the Overlap

I have written about people who by their human nature are imperfect. My story and theirs is the same. We have started, but we are not finished. We are going on. As I said to Jill, 'The essential thing in the Christian life is the will to go on.'

Doctrines like atonement, redemption, justification, sanctification, repentance, regeneration and reconciliation are bed-rock principles surrounding the cross of Christ. Upon them we proceed towards perfection. But our identification is not with doctrine, but with Christ.

Identification with the indwelling Christ means that we have decided to accept ourselves as belonging to him. We have decided to be dead to our own self-interests and to be fully alive to God himself. We live, or remain a total personality, but our control centre has been radically changed. We are the same human body but our appetites and the uses of our body are set apart for the Master. We have the same human nature, but we are indwelt by the Holy Spirit, who fires us with faith and enlarges the dimensions of our lives.

This life we now live is lived by faith, not my faith, nor yours, but our Saviour's. He has entrusted to us the message and ministry of reconciliation.

He has trusted us. What a risk. Imagine it; former

slaves to sin, prisoners to self, trained and experienced in all kinds of deceit and hate, we have been given a position of privilege and power. To us, who still live in clay personalities, he has given the inheritance of his faith. The Holy Spirit brings it to us and into us and continues to unfold its treasure. The riches of his grace are revealed by one gift after another.

It is no wonder that the thief comes to steal, kill and destroy. He sees the treasure in us. We offer no difficulty to him. We are so vulnerable. The surprise is that although vulnerable, we are not defenceless. The Holy Guardian, who abides over our treasure, is on duty within. He comes to the door with a sword and resists the enemy until he flees. That is, if we let the sword strike through the door of the spoken word. John, in the spirit, saw the sword in the mouth of the mighty conqueror. It must be in the mouth of his soldier-sons if they are to overcome in the Overlap. They must speak his word in his name. To be committed to Christ is to be committed to believing his Word. We submit our minds to him and exercise our reason in submission to the Truth as it is revealed in the living Word.

Living in the Overlap is done by faith, expressed by belief. Belief is trust in the Holy Spirit, the Son and the Father. Belief usually comes in that order. In most cases that is the sequence of the revelation given to us. The Spirit comes and convicts and convinces us to confess to the Son. Jesus forgives and cleanses us and brings us to the Father. We are the Son's bride and the Father welcomes us into the family. Faith in the treasure that is within us, the power of the Holy Spirit, the love of Jesus and the peace of God, enables us to be messengers and ministers of reconciliation.

Authority that ensures victory over the world, the

flesh and the devil, can make us reckless and vain. Unfortunately, we tend to boast a great deal over a very little success. To discipline us he chastens us with what appear as 'set backs'. We dislike it, but we learn the most during those times about the true value-system of the kingdom of God. We learn what it really means to follow Jesus.

During the times we have to submit to being taken where we do not want to go, we are learning the meaning of devotional discipleship. It usually doesn't happen until we are mature enough to accept it. Jesus pleased not himself and we have to learn to follow him in that kind of total obedience. The times when we are in others' hands are the times we are likely to think we are out of God's will. Yet, afterwards we realise we were in his hands when we were in the hands of others. Our prayer, 'Not my will, thine be done', is being answered. We are in the will of God.

We have the privilege of giving ourselves to God. That means surrender of our independence. We have come into this Overlap life by choosing to serve Jesus. The decision to follow got us started. We have declared, 'I will serve ...' Yet, we are not saved to serve, we are saved to love God himself, not simply to serve him. Love is the motive, service is the means of expressing that love. Sometimes our service itself must be sacrificed in order to express our preference to God himself rather than to our work for him. In those times of surrender our oneness with God is most like the oneness of Jesus with his Father. We have an inner joy as we sense his pleasure with us. It gives us the courage to die, as well as to live.

When we experience within the Overlap the sacrificial life of holiness, living as if we belong to God and loving it, then we glow with a passion of devotion to Jesus.

Living in the Overlap is the great life. It is the love life that trusts God in everything. It is being able to believe all things do work together for good and glory. We believe not only the biblical revelation of doctrine and the glorious revelation of the power of Jesus, but we believe much more. We believe in him, no matter what happens.

We know that in the Overlap, in the state of in-between, we are no longer in the world as we were. Nor are we as we were in ourselves. Just the same, we know that coming into the Overlap has not separated us from the world, the flesh, nor the devil. They are part of our Christian life, the real life. So, there will be conflicts, troubles, clashes with the world, the flesh and at times with the devil. Everything will not always be put right. Many times our experiences will have unhappy endings. There will be what appear as unanswered prayers. We will weep over untimely deaths and losses of all kinds. There will be embarrassing defeats that we cannot explain at all.

Commitment to Christ and to life in the Overlap is not on the basis of understanding him with the intellect, but loving him with the heart. It is risky and remains a risk all our lives. There is always the chance he is going to claim something we want to keep, command us to do something we don't understand or believe, something we can't explain. What he says again and again is, 'I trust you with my treasure, my very faith, won't you trust me with yours? I've invested myself in you, committed myself to you, won't you put yourself in my hands?'

I'm trusting him, not because I understand him more. In fact, at times I understand him less. I'm trust-

Relinquishment

ing him because through the good times and the bad
I've discovered how utterly divine he is. I mean, he is
God and I love him. It is not only God in the flesh I
love, but God in the whole biblical revelation, sov-
ereign, sublime mystery that speaks to me so tenderly
that I love him enough to trust him for ever. I believe
he is trustworthy, even when I don't understand his
ways. I'm learning this not by the things that go right,
but by the things that go wrong. Especially when I go
wrong.

In fact, that is the real work, or service, he has given
us to do. Just to believe in Jesus, whom the Father has
sent.

Life in the Overlap begins with a belief in him. It
starts and stalls according to our believing all the way
towards the high noon brilliance of the full blaze in
the biblical revelation. If our believing is only a state
of mind, then we will stop when we are depressed.
There are shadows of death and evil in our life in the
Overlap. When we step into them our minds are shadowed. If our believing streams from the inner life of
the spirit, then we will be courageous, for we will see
he is there with us in the shadows. We fear no evil.

Our confidence is in the Lord. How assuring to love
someone who believes in us. We can withstand circumstances. We shall not be crushed. We sing for we
are loved for ever. What a big life it is . . . here in the
Overlap.

A guide to life in the Overlap

Chapter Two: REVELATION

1st Day PRAYER FOR REVELATION KNOWLEDGE
Eph. 1: 16–19   Col. 1: 9–12

2nd Day REVELATION IS GIVEN BY THE HOLY SPIRIT
John 14: 26; 15: 26;   1 Cor. 2: 6–16   1 John 2: 27
  16: 13–15   Eph. 3: 3–6

3rd Day REVELATION OF THE GODHEAD THROUGH THE INCARNATION
Matt. 11: 27; 16: 15–17   2 Cor. 4: 6   Col. 1: 15
John 1: 18; 14: 7–11   Eph. 1: 17   1 John 1: 1–3

4th Day REVELATION KNOWLEDGE LEADS TO SPIRITUAL LIFE AND GROWTH
John 1: 12–13   Eph. 2: 4–5   Jas. 1: 21
2 Cor. 3: 17   Col. 3: 9–10   1 Pet. 1: 23

5th Day REVELATION KNOWLEDGE NEEDED TO RECEIVE THE GOSPEL
Rom. 1: 16–17; 16: 25–7   Eph. 3: 4–6   1 Pet. 1: 10–12

    REVELATION KNOWLEDGE NEEDED BECAUSE OF LACK OF RECOGNITION OF
    CHRIST
John 1: 10–11; 3: 3, 6, 19;   John 8: 14, 19   Eph. 4: 18
  12: 37–40   2 Cor. 4: 4

6th Day REVELATION KNOWLEDGE NEEDED TO UNDERSTAND THE WORLD

The world of nature   *The world of people*
Gen. 1: 1   John 1: 10–11; 3: 16
Ps. 24: 1   John 4: 42
Heb. 11: 3   2 Cor. 5: 19
                                     1 John 2: 2

The world of things   *The world of invisible forces and systems*
Matt. 6: 19–20   Matt. 13: 38–9   Eph. 2: 2; 6: 12
Luke 9: 25; 12: 22–31   John 10: 10; 12: 31   Col. 1: 16
1 Cor. 7: 29–31   John 14: 30; 16: 11   Rev. 12: 10
1 Tim. 6: 7–10   2 Cor. 7: 4; 11: 14
Jas. 4: 4
1 John 2: 15–17

7th Day REVELATION KNOWLEDGE IS SPIRITUAL LIGHT AND SIGHT
Luke 2: 29–32   2 Cor. 4: 6   Eph. 5: 8–9
John 1: 4, 5, 9; 8: 12

1st Day REDEMPTION – PROMISED IN THE OLD TESTAMENT, FULFILLED IN THE NEW

Old Testament

Gen. 3: 15
Gen. 49: 10
Ps. 16: 10
Ps. 22: 6–8
Ps. 22: 16
Ps. 22: 18
Ps. 27: 12
Ps. 34: 20
Ps. 41: 9
Ps. 68: 18
Ps. 69: 4, 21
Isa. 7: 14
Isa. 9: 1–2
Isa. 11: 2
Isa. 50: 6
Isa. 53: 3
Isa. 53: 4, 5
Isa. 53: 7
Isa. 53: 9
Isa. 53: 12
Micah 5: 2
Zech. 11: 12–13
Zech. 12: 10

New Testament

Gal. 4: 4
Matt. 1: 1, 6
Matt. 28: 9
Matt. 27: 39, 40, 43
John 20: 24
Mark 15: 24
Matt. 26: 60–61
John 19: 33
Mark 14. 10
Luke 24: 50–51
John 15: 23–5; 19: 29
Matt. 1: 18
Matt. 4: 12–16
Luke 2: 52
Mark 14: 65
John 1: 11; 5: 43
Matt. 8: 16–17
Matt. 26: 62–3
Matt. 27: 57–60
Matt. 27: 38
Matt. 2: 1
Matt. 26: 15; 27: 6, 7
John 19: 34

2nd Day REDEMPTION – GOD'S ANSWER

To the Sin problem

John 8: 24, 34–6; 15: 22
Rom. 3: 23–6; 5: 5, 6: 20–1
Rom. 7: 14, 21–5; 8: 2–3
Eph. 1: 3–8
Col. 1: 13–14
1 Tim. 1: 15
2 Tim. 1: 9–10
Heb. 11: 17–18
Jas. 4: 17
1 John 3: 4–5

To the Satan problem

Gen. 1: 2; 2: 8; 3: 1–7, 14–15
Isa. 45: 18; 59: 6
Matt. 25: 41–6
Luke 10: 18
John 8: 44; 12: 31–2
2 Cor. 11: 3, 14
Col. 1: 16
Heb. 2: 2, 14
1 John 3: 8
Rev. 9: 11; 12: 9–11

3rd Day REDEMPTION – GOD'S ANSWER TO MAN'S IRRESPONSIBILITY

Gen. 1: 26, 28, 31; 2: 7–9, 15–17, 20–5; 3: 1–19
Prov. 28: 13
Luke 15: 22
John 15: 22
Rom. 14: 23
Eph. 5: 6
Heb. 2: 2–3
Jas. 1: 13–14; 4: 17
1 John 1: 8–10; 3: 4

REDEMPTION – GOD'S ANSWER TO SPIRITUAL DEATH AND SEPARATION

Gen. 2: 17; 3: 8–9
Isa. 59: 1–2
Ezek. 18: 20
Luke 9: 20
John 3: 19
Rom. 1: 28–32; 5: 12, 14, 17
Rom. 6: 16, 23; 8: 6, 18
Eph. 2: 1
Heb. 2: 14
Jas. 1: 15; 5: 20

4th Day REDEMPTION – ACCOMPLISHED THROUGH THE ATONEMENT

Gen. 3: 21; 4: 4; 6: 5–8; 8: 20–2
Gen. 12: 1–3, 7, 8, 13–18; 22: 1–9
Exod. 1: 8–14; 11: 4–7; 12: 1–13
John 1: 29; 19: 36
Rom. 4: 7–8; 5: 8–9; 6: 23
Heb. 9: 28; 10: 1–14

4th Day – continued

Exod. 20: 24–6; 24: 3–8
Lev. 4: 20; 16: 20–2 30; 17: 11
Isa. 53: 6
Heb. 8: 5–6; 9: 18–22; 11: 24–8

Heb. 11: 4–9, 17–19
1 Cor. 2: 2; 5: 7–8; 6: 19–20
Eph. 1: 7; 5: 2
1 Pet. 1: 18–19

REDEMPTION – ACCOMPLISHED BY THE REDEEMER

Mark 10: 45
Luke 2: 18; 4: 18; 19: 10
John 1: 9, 29; 8: 24; 17: 4
Rom. 3: 24

1 Cor. 1: 30
Eph. 1, 17
1 Tim. 2: 5–6
Titus 2: 14

Heb. 9: 12
1 Pet. 1: 18–20
Rev. 5: 9–10

REDEMPTION – COMPLETED AT THE CROSS

Matt. 26: 17–18, 28;
27:46–50
Luke 9: 31; 22: 53; 23: 25
John 3: 14; 12: 27–31;
  14: 30

Acts 4: 27–8
Rom. 5: 6–9
1 Cor. 1: 17–18; 15: 3

2 Tim. 1: 10
Heb. 2: 9–15; 9: 26–8
Heb. 13: 20–1

5th Day   REDEMPTION – RECONCILES ALIENATED MAN TO GOD

Gen. 3: 8–9, 24
Isa. 59: 1–2; 53: 6

Rom. 5: 10–11
Col. 1: 20–2

Heb. 10: 14, 22
1 Pet. 2: 25

6th Day   REDEMPTION – RELEASES THE CAPTIVE

Prov. 5: 22
Isa. 61: 1
Luke 4: 18; 13: 16
John 8: 34

Acts 10: 38; 13: 38–9
Rom. 5: 1–2; 6: 14,
  16–18, 20, 23
Rom. 7: 14, 23–5; 8: 2–4

Eph. 4: 8–9
Col. 1: 13–14; 2: 15
Heb. 2: 14–15
1 Pet. 3: 18–19

7th Day   REDEMPTION – VICTORY OVER DEATH, HELL AND GRAVE

Isa. 53: 9, 12
Ps. 16: 10; 68: 18
Matt. 12: 40; 16: 21;
  28: 5-7

Luke 24: 50–1
John 12: 30–1
Acts 1: 9; 2: 24, 31

Heb. 2: 14
1 John 3: 8
Rev. 12: 9–12

Chapter Six: REGENERATION

1st Day   REGENERATION – RESULT OF REDEMPTION

Matt. 1: 21
John 1: 29
Rom. 6: 6; 8: 3

1 Cor. 1: 18
Gal. 6: 14; 2: 20
Eph. 1: 5–8

Phil. 4: 5–8
Col. 1: 13–14
1 Pet. 1: 18–19

2nd Day   REGENERATION COMES THROUGH REVELATION KNOWLEDGE

Matt. 16 16–17

John 16: 7–14; 15: 26

1 Cor. 2: 9–13

3rd Day   REGENERATION – OBTAINED BY REPENTANCE

Ps. 32: 5
Matt. 3: 8; 16: 16
Luke 5: 8; 15: 18

John 20: 28–9
Acts 2: 38–9; 3: 9
Acts 8: 22; 11: 18

Rom. 2: 4–5; 10: 9–13
1 Tim. 6: 12–13

4th Day   REGENERATION IS NEW BIRTH BY THE HOLY SPIRIT

John 3: 3–8; 6: 63
Rom. 8: 14–17
2 Cor. 5: 17; 3: 3, 6

Eph. 1: 5
1 Pet. 1: 23
2 Pet. 1: 4

Titus 3: 5
1 John 4: 7; 5: 1–5

5th Day REGENERATION IS TRANSITION

Death to Life

John 3: 5, 6, 16; 1: 12, 13
John 5: 24; 10: 10; 11: 25
Rom. 6: 4–8
1 Cor. 6: 17; 15: 22
Gal. 2: 20
Eph. 2: 1–5; 4: 18–23
Col. 2: 13
Phil. 1: 21
1 Pet. 1: 3, 23
1 John 3: 14; 5. 12

Lost to Found

Isa. 53: 6
Luke 19: 10; 15: 24
1 Pet. 2: 25

6th Day REGENERATION IS TRANSITION

Darkness to Light

Prov. 4: 18
John 1: 4–5
Acts 26: 18
2 Cor. 4: 6
Col. 1: 12–14
1 Pet. 2: 9

Blindness to Sight

Luke 10: 21
John 3: 3
2 Cor. 3: 16–18; 4: 3–4
Eph. 1: 17–18

7th Day REGENERATION IS TRANSITION

Condemnation to Justification (Guilty to Not Guilty)

John 8: 36
Rom. 3: 23, 24; 4: 24–5; 5: 8–11
Rom. 8: 1–2, 15, 33–4
1 Cor. 6: 9–11

2 Cor. 3: 17; 5: 21
Phil. 3. 9–10
Titus 3: 3–7
1 Pet. 2: 24

Chapter Eight: RECOGNITION

1st Day RECOGNITION DEVELOPS DISCERNMENT

Prov. 4: 18   1 Cor. 2: 10–16   Eph. 1: 16–20; 2: 10
Luke 10: 21

DISCERNMENT OF THE WORLD

World of nature	*World of people*	*World of things*
Ps. 24: 1	John 3: 12; 4: 42	Matt. 4: 8; 5: 12–14
John 1: 10	John 17: 11–18	Rom. 12: 2
Acts 17: 24	Titus 2: 11–14	1 Cor. 2: 22–3
Rom. 8: 16–18		Gal. 6: 14
Col. 1: 16–18		1 John 2: 15–17; 5: 4, 5, 19
2 Pet. 3: 5, 7, 13		

DISCERNMENT OF HOSTILE WORLD OF EVIL SYSTEMS

Matt. 5: 13–16   2 Cor. 2: 11; 4: 4   2 Thess. 2: 9–10
John 3: 19; 14: 30–1;   Eph. 2: 3; 6: 12   2 Tim. 2: 26
   15: 18–19; 17: 16

2nd Day RECOGNITION DEVELOPS DISCERNMENT OF THE FLESH AND THE DEVIL

Flesh (Carnality)

Rom. 6: 1–2, 12; 8: 7–8
1 Cor. 3: 3
2 Cor. 10: 4
Col. 3: 1–3
1 Pet. 4: 1–2
1 John 2: 16–17

Devil

Mark 4: 15
Luke 10: 18; 11: 14–18
Luke 13: 16; 22: 31
John 8: 44; 16: 11
Acts 5: 3
Eph. 4: 27; 6: 11
1 Pet. 5: 8
Rev. 12: 9; 20: 10

Justified

Rom. 3: 23–6; 5: 1–2, 8, 11; 8: 31–4
Gal. 5: 1
Titus 3: 3–7

Sanctified

John 17: 16–19
Acts 26: 18
Rom. 6: 1–11, 17–19
1 Cor. 1: 30–1
1 Thess. 5: 23
2 Thess. 2: 13
Heb. 2: 11–13; 10: 14

3rd Day   RECOGNITION OF VICTORY

The Victory of Jesus

Gen. 3: 15
Matt. 12: 28
Luke 4: 1–14; 11: 20–2
John 12: 31–2; 16: 11
Acts 10: 38
1 Cor. 15: 24–6
Phil. 2: 9–11
Heb. 2: 14–15
2 Pet. 2: 4–10
1 John 3: 8
Rev. 17: 14

Our Victory in him

Mark 16: 15–18
Luke 10: 19–22
John 14: 12–13; 17: 18
Rom. 16: 20
1 Cor. 10: 13; 15: 57
Col. 2: 10, 13–15
2 Tim. 1: 7
Heb. 2: 15
1 John 4: 4; 5: 4–5
Rev. 2: 7; 3: 5, 12
Rev. 12: 7–11

4th Day   RECOGNITION OF OUR SPIRITUAL WEAPONS

The Word

Matt. 4: 4
John 6: 63; 15: 3, 26
John 17: 8, 17
Eph. 6: 17
Heb. 4: 11–12
Isa. 49: 2
Rev. 1: 16

The Blood

Zech. 9: 11
Acts 20: 28
Rom. 5: 9
Col. 1: 20–2
Heb. 9: 7, 14, 22
Heb. 11: 27; 12: 24
1 John 1: 7
Rev. 5: 9, 10; 7: 14; 12: 11

The Holy Spirit

Matt. 3: 11
Luke 11: 13; 24: 49
Luke 12: 12
John 14: 26
Acts 1: 8
Acts 2: 4; 4: 33
1 Cor, 2: 4
Eph. 3: 16, 20

The Name

Luke 24: 47
John 14: 13; 15; 16; 16: 26
Acts 3: 6, 16; 16: 18
Phil. 2: 9–11
Rev. 19: 16

5th Day   RECOGNITION OF THE CAUSES OF OUR CONFLICTS

Luke 16: 13
John 16: 33
Rom. 8: 35–9; 6: 12–14,
  19; 7: 21–2

2 Cor. 5: 19
1 Cor. 3: 3
2 Cor. 1: 4–10; 2: 8–11
2 Cor. 4: 7–11, 16–18

Eph. 6: 12
1 Tim. 1: 18–20; 6: 9–12
2 Tim. 2: 4–6

6th Day   RECOGNITION OF OUR POSITION IN CHRIST

Sons

John 8: 34–6
Rom. 8: 14–17
1 Cor. 6: 17; 8: 5–6
Gal. 4: 3–9
Eph. 1: 4–6; 2: 19

Soldiers

Ps. 44: 5
Luke 10: 19
Rom. 8: 35–8
2 Cor. 6: 7; 10: 3–6
Eph. 3: 10; 6: 10–18

Priests

Matt. 16: 18–19
John 20: 21–2
1 Cor. 2: 12; 3: 16; 12: 1
2 Cor. 3: 6
Eph. 2: 1, 4, 6

6th Day – continued

Sons	Soldiers	Priests
2 Pet. 1: 4	1 Thess. 5: 8	Heb. 3: 1; 4: 14–16
1 John 5: 1	Heb. 4: 11	1 Pet. 2: 9
	Jas. 4: 7	1 John 5: 14–15
	1 Pet. 5: 8–9	Rev. 1: 5–6

7th Day   RECOGNITION LEADS US TOWARDS GLORIFICATION

1 Cor. 6: 2–3; 15: 57–8   2 Thess. 2: 13–14   Rev. 2: 7, 25–6; 3: 5, 12;
1 Thess. 5: 23–4   17: 14

Chapter Ten: RECONCILIATION

1st Day   RECONCILIATION – MESSAGE AND MINISTRY

The Message	*The Ministry of Love*
John 5: 24; 6: 63; 8: 32; 10: 10; 17: 8	Matt. 22: 36–9
Acts 5: 20; 2: 37–41	Luke 10: 34
Rom. 4: 7–8; 5: 10–11; 10: 8–17	Rom. 15: 1–3
1 Cor. 2: 1–5	1 Cor. 16: 14
2 Cor. 5: 19–20	Eph. 6: 6–8
Eph. 2: 14	Jas. 5: 19–20
	1 Pet. 3: 9
	1 John 4: 11–12

The Ministry of self-sacrifice

Matt. 16: 25	1 Cor. 9: 19–23; 4: 13
Acts 20: 24	2 Cor. 4: 5; 6: 4–10

2nd Day   RECONCILIATION – GOD'S LOVE COVERS OUR SHAME

Gen. 3: 8–9, 21	Rom. 4: 7–8; 5: 8–9;	Heb. 2: 14–15; 9: 14
Ps. 44: 15	8: 1, 31, 34	1 John 3: 20
Luke 15: 21–2		

RECONCILIATION – THROUGH CHRIST'S ATONEMENT

Exod. 17: 11	Eph. 5: 2	1 John 3: 16
Isa. 53: 7	Col. 1: 20	Rev. 5: 9–10; 7: 14;
John 19: 34	1 Pet. 1: 18–19, 22	12: 11
1 Cor. 5: 6–8		

3rd Day   RECONCILIATION – WE FORGIVE BECAUSE HE FORGAVE

Matt. 5: 43–5; 6: 14	Eph. 4: 32	1 Pet. 3: 9
Mark 11: 25		

RECONCILIATION PRODUCES FELLOWSHIP

Eccles. 4: 9–12	Matt. 11: 29–30	Col. 3: 12–17
Mal. 3: 16	Acts 2: 36–42	1 John 1: 7–9

4th Day   RECONCILIATION – MINISTRY OF GOD'S FAMILY, THE BELIEVER PRIESTHOOD

Rom. 15: 5–6, 15–16	Col. 3: 1, 12, 25	1 Pet. 2: 4, 9–10
Eph. 5: 2; 2: 4–7	Heb. 8: 1; 10: 19–25	1 John 3: 16–18

5th Day   RECONCILIATION – MINISTRY OF POWER AND AUTHORITY

Matt. 18: 18–20	Acts 1: 8; 2: 2–4; 3: 6–16	Phil. 2: 9–13
Mark 16: 15–20	1 Cor. 4: 20; 6: 7	Jas. 3: 5
Luke 10: 19	2 Cor. 5: 20; 6: 3–7	1 Pet. 2: 9–10; 4: 10
John 14: 12–16; 17:18;	Eph. 1: 3, 17–19; 3: 20–1	
20: 21		

6th Day   RECONCILIATION – MINISTRY OF DELIVERANCE

Rom. 8: 15–17; 15: 30–3   Phil. 1: 19–20   Jas. 5: 14–16
1 Cor. 1: 8–11; 4: 7–12;   Philemon 20   1 Pet. 1: 22
  7: 5–10

7th Day   RECONCILIATION – RESULT OF REPENTANCE

Ps. 19: 12; 40: 12; 51: 3   Matt. 26: 75   John 8: 9–11; 13: 8–9
Ps. 38   Luke 5: 8; 15: 17–21;
Prov. 28: 13   22: 31–3; 24: 34
Isa. 6: 5–8

Chapter Twelve: RELINQUISHMENT

1st Day   RELINQUISHMENT – ACCEPTANCE OF LIFE IN THE OVERLAP

Ps. 23: 4   Phil. 2: 15; 3: 8, 12–16   1 Pet. 1: 3–9; 4: 12;
John 11: 3, 6, 15, 25;   Heb. 11: 13–16; 12: 1–4   5: 6–11
  16: 22   Jas. 1: 2–3; 4: 6–7

2nd Day   RELINQUISHMENT IS SURRENDER TO THE FATHER'S WILL

Isa. 55: 6–9   Eph. 5: 8–10   Heb. 5: 8–9; 12: 5–11
Matt. 6: 10   Phil. 2: 3–8   1 Pet. 2: 21
Mark 14: 36

3rd Day   RELINQUISHMENT IS HAVING FAITH IN JESUS

John 5: 39–40; 6: 29   Phil. 3: 7–10   1 Pet. 1: 8–9
Gal. 2: 20   Heb. 12: 2–3   1 John 5: 4–5
Eph. 2: 8–9

4th Day   RELINQUISHMENT IS LOVING GOD MORE THAN ALL ELSE

Matt. 22: 37–8   Rom. 8: 28   Eph. 6: 6
John 21: 5   1 Cor. 2: 9   Jas. 1: 12

5th Day   RELINQUISHMENT IS OUR RESPONSE TO GOD'S TRUST IN US

Acts 20: 24   1 Cor. 1: 26–31   2 Cor. 5: 18–20
Rom. 11: 29, 33–9

6th Day   RELINQUISHMENT IS SECRET OF POWER TO HOLD ON

2 Cor. 4: 1, 16   Jas. 1: 2–4, 12   1 Pet. 4: 12–14
2 Tim. 1: 12

RELINQUISHMENT IS THE SECRET OF FAITH TO LET GO

Let go of self-dependence   *Let go our physical selves*

Ps. 37: 5   Ps. 139: 13–18
John 5: 5–6; 21: 18–19   Rom. 14: 8; 12: 1–2
Rom. 8: 5, 8, 14   1 Cor. 6: 19–20
1 Cor. 1: 30–1

Let go our personal selves

Matt. 16: 24–5
Luke 1: 38; 23: 46
Acts 7: 59
Rom. 6: 6–8, 11
Col. 3: 3
1 Pet. 4: 19

7th Day   RELINQUISHMENT REVEALS GOD'S WORK IN US

John 15: 2   2 Cor. 4: 7   Phil. 2: 13
1 Cor. 1: 4–9   Eph. 4: 19